A Must Read

- If you drink and sometimes can't remember...
- If you live with or know someone who blacks out...
- If you ride in a car driven by such a person...
- If you are a policeman or paramedic dealing with him...
- If you are a doctor or nurse in an emergency room...
- If you are a lawyer prosecuting or defending a blacked out person.

You Will Learn

- How to recognize the blacked out person is unconscious and has no idea what he or she is doing...
- How to cope with him or her...
- How to protect the blacked out person and yourself from harm...
- How to drink to prevent blackouts...
- Why blackouts are a huge, misunderstood and unrecognized problem for the Law and Society.
- And Much More.

What Others Say

"I've been clean 16-plus years. At the time I went sober I was an undercover vice cops. Blackouts were quite the norm for those days. Where's my car? Who are you young lady and is this your bedroom? Why does my snub nose have three spent rounds in the chamber? The Alcohol Blackout brought back frightening memories. A must read for those who want to understand the insanity."

"During a blackout you can do ANYTHING, drive, make love, get married and/or commit murder—and never know you did it. And that time period can last for DAYS—for Real!! "Get this book!"

"When Dr. Sweeney says a person in a blackout cannot form intent, it is nothing less than a revolution in criminal justice."

"This book is filled with horrendous case histories. They walk and talk, drive and quarrel and get into fights. They are a bloody menace."

"I found the book fascinating. The idea that a blacked out person is compromised with no short term memory is a very important one."

"Dr. Sweeney is absolutely correct when he asserts that alcohol blackouts are understudied and that they occur more often than most people think."

"I don't remember how we left, how we got home, if I brought my purse, if I made out with strangers, if we had sex...So I wake up this morning and I'm walking around finding clues."

"I have a few instances where I have been told I am awake and coherent but have no recollection of what occurred. I'm terrified."

"I was especially attracted to the info on how to recognize when a person is in a black-out and how to deal with him."

"You are the first person I have ever found that truly has saved me from myself. I am scared. I know what it is to wake up in the morning with the feeling that I hurt someone...I had my dads gun...from his apartment....don't know how I got it. I thought I killed him."

THE ALCOHOL BLACKOUT

Walking, Talking, Unconscious... and Lethal

Donal F. Sweeney, M.D.

With

Robert A. Liston

MP

Mnemosyne Press, Santa Barbara

Mnemosyne Press
222 West Anapamu Street, Suite 7
Santa Barbara CA 93101
805-962-4929

P.O. Box 3276
Santa Barbara, CA 93130

AlcoholBlackout.com

Catalog-in-publication data is on file with the

Library of Congress

IBSN: 0-9747943-090000

10 9 8 7 6 5 4 3 2

Cover Design: Tim Gray. Illustrations: Ryan Lonac. Book Design: Bob Faulkner

Contents

Acknowledgements vii
Foreword 1
Ask a Simple Question 1
1 Three Lost Days 5
2 Where Are My Clothes? 14
3 Life In The Perpetual Present 20
4 "Did Anyone Get Anything To Eat?" 30
5 Ether's First Cousin 39
6 "What's a Blackout?" 44
7 Living With Blackouts 57
8 Recognizing The Blackout 66
9 Three Little Words 71
10 Are They Conscious? 78
11 Dr. Jekyll Meet Mr. Hyde 92
12 If Only The Jury Had Heard... 105
13 Only In His Dreams 118
14 Throw Away The Key 129
15 A Promising Start 139
16 Falling Through The Cracks 152
17 An Open Door 161
Appendix 164
Other Blackout Drugs 164
Sources 173
About the Authors 179

All my life I loved one woman.
It took me years to find her–
but find her I did.
And it is to Jo
That I dedicate this book.

THANK YOU

For Reading My Book

THE ALCOHOL BLACKOUT!

I value your opinion

Please send comments to

sweeney@alcoholblackout.com

Donal F. Sweeney, M.D.

Acknowledgements

It is impossible in this short space to mention all those who have contributed to this book. But I simply must acknowledge the following:

My parents, Eugene and Betty—a love of reading and a continuous curiosity.

My primary school teachers, from Sister Hyacinth to Brother Perry, who always encouraged me to "look it up."

In college and medical school, my teachers like Professor Murtaugh and gastroenterologist Marty Finkel—who wouldn't give me answers, but said answers were there.

In the US Air Force Medical Service great teachers such as Doctors Stonehill, Nareff, Philippi, who all taught me to make it happen.

My friends who saved my own memory—in the great recovery community, like Brian, Jenn, Peter, Alex and a host of others.

My colleague, Jim Wells, who always encouraged problem solving.

My children and grandchildren who gave me the opportunity to observe the incredible human brain "turning on and developing."

NASA's Jet Propulsion Lab, where I was privileged to watch fellow scientists like Ed Stone and engineers like Tom Gavin solve whatever problems seem to arise.

All the thinkers and researchers in the multiple areas of addiction medicine, anesthesia, psychology and psychiatry, neuroscience who pioneered the work that helped synthesize this story of the search for the blackout phenomena.

To my psychologist son, Doctor Daniel aka Danny and my good friend Alex Brumbaugh, who acted as skeptics, critics and advisors, and especially to my friend and writer Bob Liston.

Quite a ride!

D.F.S., M.D.
Santa Barbara, California

Foreword
Ask a Simple Question

Looking back on it, the date should be cemented in my memory, but it is not. The best I can remember is that it was sometime in the mid-1980s when a question changed my life.

I was lecturing on alcoholism at the University of California at Santa Barbara when a young man stood up and asked, "What's a blackout?"*

I don't remember my answer, but I'm sure it was something lame to mask my ignorance. The truth is I didn't know, and I was embarrassed. Here I was, a doctor of internal medicine, board certified in addictive medicine, giving a lecture on alcoholism at a major university, and I couldn't explain one of the more common manifestations of alcohol abuse.

I set out to find an answer. It didn't figure to be a tough question, just something I'd overlooked. Surely the alcohol blackout had been studied and explained.

I started with medical textbooks. Many ignored the subject or gave only vague and extremely limited references. Attempts

---

*The term is unfortunate, especially when it also refers to an outage by the electric utility company. A better term for this book might be "blankout," but I fear we are stuck with blackout.

to simply define a blackout were all over the place, with as many definitions as there were people to make them. All definitions appeared to include an element of guesswork. I discovered that very little research on blackouts was being done. Most of what had occurred came in the late 1960s.

Very early on I was forced to an obvious conclusion: nobody really knew much about blackouts. Nor were very many people trying to learn. One of the more common neurological dysfunctions–blacking out and not remembering, while consuming a common and legal substance–had somehow fallen through the cracks of medicine and science.

Later on in this book, I will discuss how that may have happened. But it may be said upfront: it shouldn't have happened and it can't be allowed to persist.

That young man asked a legitimate question. There had to be an answer. At least there ought to be. My search took me far afield from internal medicine or addiction medicine. I was forced to delve into neurology, neuroscience, psychiatry, psychology, pharmacology, anesthesiology and other specialties. My search for answers meant inquiries into memory and its function, into consciousness and its nature. I was even required to study the law, forensics and police tactics, all places doctors of internal medicine seldom enter.

No answer existed when I began my studies, but it came quickly. Almost every issue of medical and scientific journals, it seemed, offered new insight into brain function, memory and consciousness. Using modern equipment such as MRI and PET scans, scientists began opening up the secrets of the brain rapidly.

I should point out that none of these people were studying blackouts *per se*. They were trying to find out how the brain works, still a major scientific inquiry. What I have done is apply these studies of memory, consciousness and other brain functions to blackouts.

The more we learn the more there is to learn. But, the answer to that young man's question is at hand. We know what a blackout is. We have a pretty good idea what causes it and how it might be prevented. We know the blackout is a far more serious condition than heretofore thought. We know the desperate need for further study.

If I have made a contribution, it is in realizing that if a person in a blackout has stopped forming memory–now widely accepted theory–then that person is in an unconscious state. He has no idea what he is doing. He is out of control. For blacked out men and women to walk, talk, drive, get into arguments, pick fights and become violent while unconscious is an intolerable situation.

In writing this book I am treading on some medical and scientific toes, I know. I can already hear the questions: Who does this guy think he is? What does this internist, a glorified GP, know about neurotransmitters and anterograde amnesia?

The obvious answer is not enough. I am still reading, learning. But we must begin somewhere, sometime. How many more car crashes, murders and forms of mayhem must occur in blackouts while scientists and medical doctors argue about whose turf is being invaded and who has the superior knowledge?

I can also hear another question. Rather than urging others to perform research into blackouts, why don't I do it myself? The answer is: Don't I wish! By the time that young man asked his question and I'd found even a partial answer, any chance for me to set up a lab and obtain grants was past.

My career path had taken me into the Air Force from medical school, then into private practice, then to the Jet Propulsion Laboratory. Early on I specialized in chest medicine, later on in addiction medicine. I have been and am (even in semi-retirement) a physician–albeit one who loves problem solving.

So, I must ask others to research what I cannot. I hope they will not mind an idea or two, even a suggestion.

Finally, I want to urge readers to send me their experiences with blackouts. I will not be able to acknowledge most of the stories, but they will contribute to our knowledge. Postal and Internet addresses are on the copyright page.

1
Three Lost Days

On July 2, 1995, a Sunday, Kevin Price drove from his home in Hoboken to the New Jersey shore to celebrate the Fourth of July weekend with friends.

Drinking was well underway when he arrived around midnight. He may have played catch-up, perhaps swilling beers too fast. He remembers playing a chug-a-lug game called "quarters."* What harm? They were all spending the night. No one was to drive. The host's father attended the party. It was a safe time to drink. They indeed did.

Around 2:30 a.m. or so, Price felt a little sick to his stomach and went to the bathroom. No one paid attention to him, and quite some time passed before someone asked, "Where's Kevin?" No one could find him and his car was gone. Maybe he went home. Someone phoned there about 4 a.m. to inquire. No, Kevin hadn't come home.

Those best able to answer the "Where's Kevin?" question were motorists on the Garden State Parkway. About 4 a.m. they saw the headlights of a car heading south, the wrong way, in the north-

*The object is to bounce a quarter coin off a table or counter top into a glass of beer. If the player misses he must down the beer.

bound lanes. They blinked their lights, blew their horns, waved, shouted as they evaded his car. Kevin was oblivious.

Along came a van carrying six people, returning from the casinos in Atlantic City. Either the van driver didn't see Kevin's car or he couldn't avoid it.

Just south of the Raritan South tollbooth, the two vehicles collided head-on. The van burst into flames. Four people perished in the conflagration, another died at the hospital. Only the two drivers survived.*

What makes this case different from a jillion other drunk driving tragedies?

Kevin Price wasn't just drunk, he had *blacked out.* He had not *passed out,* that is, fallen asleep in an alcoholic stupor. He was awake. He walked, he talked, obviously he could drive his car. But *he does not remember doing any of it.* He vaguely recalls being in the bathroom at his friend's house. The next thing he remembers is waking up in a hospital room and asking his uncle where he was. It was three days later.

Blacking out is a common and frequent effect of alcohol. It has been going on for thousands of years. But only recently have we come to understand what happens to Kevin Price and all the millions of others who have memory loss when they drink.

Kevin Price did not have amnesia. He did not *forget* what happened during those three lost days–three days for which he was sentenced to up to 21 years in prison for aggravated vehicular manslaughter, three days which remain a huge, gaping hole in his

*Declared dead at the scene were Evelyn Dotson, 80; Henrietta E. Lathan, 73; Jeanne Ruth Sandford, 69; and Gwendolyn King, 62. Mrs. Johnny Ruth Buie, wife of Matthrew Buie, driver of the van, died at the hospital. The New York Times de-scribed all as "tireless volunteers" and "vital energy" at the 50-member St. Augustine Church in Patterson, NJ, itself "an oasis of stability and hope in a neighborhood where hope is often all but lost." Their deaths truly compound a ghastly tragedy.

young life. He will not recall later under hypnosis or some kind of "truth serum." He did not engage in Freudian repression of an unpleasant event. He is not lying or malingering in an effort to escape the consequences of his actions.

We now know Kevin Price does not remember because he never formed any memory from the time he stood in that bathroom until he woke up in the hospital bed. He was blacked out.

Not forming memories is vastly different from knowing something and forgetting it. Even if we later forget what we heard, saw or thought, we at least know it at the appropriate time to make proper use of the information.

Because he could not form memory, Price was living in the precise present. What he might have seen, heard, or felt a moment, a minute or five minutes ago was unknown to him.

Without memory of what had just happened, he could not make use of past knowledge to alter his conduct. For example, he was eminently capable of repeating himself over and over without realizing it. Much worse, his past knowledge that he should not drink and drive had no way to impact his consciousness.

He was out of control, wholly impulsive. Without knowledge of recent events, he had no capacity for rational thought. He was incapable of considering the consequences of his actions or knowing what he was doing beyond the immediate moment. He was the proverbial loose cannon, and in the car, a menace to himself and others.

Memory formation is so much a part of who we are and what we do, it is almost impossible to imagine life without it. Kevin Price was talking without knowing what he was saying, walking without knowing where he was going–and driving with no destination.

Kevin Price was unconscious.

Many have tried to figure out what was going on in the head of Kevin Price, including family, friends, police, defense attorneys, judge and Kevin himself. I even had a hand in it as a consultant for his defense team. And, the figuring out is important, for the tragic events of that summer night may help us understand the phenomena known as blackouts.

Kevin Price came from a good family in New Jersey. He was 24, a graduate of Bucknell University, and at the time worked in the financial district of Manhattan. He had a steady girlfriend. If there was anything remarkable in the life of Kevin Price it was his status as among the best and brightest of our young people.

Kevin was not an alcoholic in any but the most restricted meaning of the word. He was a party boy, hardly some besotted toper having DTs while begging for his next drink. His driving record shows a couple of speeding tickets, but no DUI arrest.

I asked Kevin if he had ever blacked out before? Was it a problem for him? He said he had fallen asleep at a traffic light once and a motorist behind him blew his horn. In college he fell asleep on the lawn outside the dorm. Both of these suggest pass outs, falling asleep from alcohol sedation. They bear no resemblance to the blackout he suffered that July night, a special and specific type of brain dysfunction. With no previous experience, he had no way to anticipate a blackout. The thought of one never occurred to him.

Independence Day came on a Tuesday in 1995, creating a long weekend for Kevin. He and his girlfriend spent Saturday and most of Sunday with friends at a cabin on a lake in New Jersey. Along with boating and swimming, a good bit of drinking occurred.

Kevin didn't have to work on Monday, but his girlfriend did. So, on Sunday evening he drove her back to his place in Hoboken, which lies across the Hudson River from midtown Manhattan. She would work the next day, then take the train down on Tuesday to join him. When she answered the phone at 4 a.m. Monday, she thought his friends were joking and went back to sleep. She boarded the train later that next morning, arriving to discover the disaster that had befallen Kevin. There had been no joke.

These events raise the question of the role of fatigue in blackouts. Anyone who has ever imbibed too much can attest to the effects of alcohol on sleep. The person enters a period of deep, dreamless sleep lasting perhaps three hours or so. When the worst effects of the alcohol wear off, the person awakens, perhaps not to go back to sleep at all. If he does sleep, it is often greatly disturbed, fitful, and marked by headaches, dry mouth and other manifestations of a hangover.

This person does not get sufficient rest, although he may lie in bed several hours. If he imbibes the next day, the celebrated "hair of the dog" to relieve his hangover, he may feel more alert for a while. But his underlying fatigue continues and worsens.

Kevin Price drank on Saturday and continued to drink on Sunday. He drove from the lake in New Jersey to Hoboken, left his girlfriend there, then drove in heavy traffic to the New Jersey shore. It is likely that fatigue contributed to his blackout.

When he arrived at the party around midnight, he began drinking beer at a rapid rate. Some accounts report that he had as many as eight or 10 beers in a few hours. Rapid consumption of alcohol may have contributed to Kevin's blackout.

And the heavy drinking comes at the end of a second day of consumption. He is young and healthy, but his body is having trouble coping with the excess of alcohol. He is in an advanced state of inebriation. He feels nauseous and goes to the bathroom.

How long he remained there is unknown. He cannot tell us. Perhaps he vomited. But at some point he emerged. No one seems to have noticed or paid much attention to him. Therefore it may be concluded that Kevin did nothing unusual. He did not rant or rave, curse, pick fights, fall down, throw up, slobber or any of the other sometimes manifestations of drunkenness.

Again, he appeared normal to the others at the party, walking and talking as he usually did. But he wasn't normal. He was in an advanced state of alcohol-induced brain dysfunction. Even if someone had remained sober–a designated driver, perhaps–that person was unlikely to notice any change in Kevin, unless she or he knew him extremely well. If they haven't been drinking too much themselves, spouses can usually tell when their mates are drunk. But even wives find it almost impossible to recognize when husbands have blacked out.

Can this be? How can it be possible for a person to walk, talk, act near normally, yet be blacked out and without conscious awareness of what he is doing?

Kevin Price was not amnesiac. He had lots of memory. He remembered all that had happened to him prior to blacking out in the bathroom, everyone he knew, all the significant events of his life. This is called episodic memory. He possessed all his education and everything he had ever learned. This is called semantic memory. And he still held on to all his procedural memory. Everything he'd ever learned to do, such as walk, talk, ride a bicycle, drive a car, still existed in his brain.

Even though he was quite drunk, Price still possessed all his senses, although in a diminished state. He saw, heard, etc. He formed thoughts based upon what he had seen or heard. But in his blacked out state, those impressions and thoughts were entirely fleeting. They remained in his head (immediate memory) until the next sense impression or distraction, a matter of moments, not more than a couple of minutes.

Said another way, the link between current and past knowledge—his short-term memory or what psychologists now call *working memory*—was broken. Without short-term or working memory, Price could not function in society except in an impulsive and superficial way.

Procedural memory allowed him to walk—and drive. He could talk, but it was not normal conversation, rather more like bantering and highly repetitious. Still, no one would have guessed he had blacked out.

What went on in the mind of Kevin Price when he came out of the bathroom? I can only guess. Kevin had felt ill, doubtlessly from too much booze. It is logical—to you and me, but nothing was logical to Kevin—that he wanted to lie down, maybe to sleep (pass out). Sleep where?

His pre-bathroom memory still functions, so he remembers bringing his sleeping bag to spend the night. He also remembers he had left it in his car. He'll go and get it. (It is agonizing to ponder what might have been prevented had Kevin carried the sleeping bag inside when he arrived.)

Kevin walks out to his sports car and opens the door with the clicker on his car keys. Again, he has no ability to form memory. He lives from moment to moment. When he arrives at the car, he has no memory of coming for his sleeping bag. He is standing there with the car door open and the keys in his hand. Why would he do that except to drive somewhere? Better said, using his keys to unlock the car, then open the door, get in, start the engine and drive somewhere is automatic for him. He has done it so many times it is embedded in his still functioning procedural memory.

I suspect Kevin Price got in his car, started the engine and drove off with no idea where he was going. He was just driving.

The elapsed time suggests he may have done so for quite some time, finally ending up on the Garden State Parkway.

Another scenario is possible. Feeling ill and sleepy, perhaps Kevin heads for home to lie down. But a moment later he will not remember making the decision or know where he is or what he's doing on the Garden State.

He drives some distance. Authorities received no reports of erratic or reckless driving, as he drove north on the Garden State, so it must be assumed Kevin drove in a near normal manner.

The police received their first report about Kevin from the operator of the Raritan South tollbooth. I assume it was to the effect that some "idiot" had passed through the tolls, then turned around, driven the wrong way through the tolls and was headed south in the north lanes. Cops responded immediately.

Why did he turn around to go back? Only God knows. Kevin can never tell us. My guess is something–perhaps a sign giving the mileage to New York, perhaps the fact of the toll booth itself–triggered Kevin's pre-blackout memory that he was supposed to spend the night at his friend's beach house.

He turns around to go back, thus creating a tragedy only Euripides could love. Why didn't he pull off the parkway, cross over and reenter the south-bound lanes? No one will ever know. But it must be assumed that Kevin, unable to form memory, did not realize he was on the Garden State and so did not conform to the rules for driving on it. A person in a blackout does not know where he or she is located on this planet.

The horrific collision does not sober up Kevin. His ability to form memory does not suddenly return. It is not like waking a sleepwalker. Within a moment, he cannot remember the crash, what happened or where he is. In pain from his broken leg, Kevin irrationally screams at and struggles with the people trying to rescue him.

Blackouts can last for several days, but such cases usually involve continued and mindless drinking. Kevin should have come out of his blackout within a few hours, but I have no doubt the sedatives and anesthesia continued it into the third day.

His family and friends learned of the accident and kept a bedside vigil. When Kevin finally awoke, his uncle was present to tell him the horrors of that night. Not very long afterward Kevin learned he was to face charges of vehicular manslaughter.

Kevin Price was sentenced to 21 years in prison. He served five years and two months, then was placed under parole supervision until January 18, 2010. He has a business selling shared ownership in single engine aircraft. He married in October 2003. Kevin speaks to youth and college age groups on the dangers of alcohol. He no longer drinks.

Price had one advantage. Because of the accident, he at least knew what he'd done while blacked out. That doesn't always happen. And not knowing and not being able to find out is the private terror of those who have blacked out. We consider this next.

2
Where Are My Clothes?

Along with the shakes, pounding head and cottonmouth, the post-blackout person must come to grips with a great big hole in his memory. Life went on for several hours and he has no awareness of it. He remembers no actions or words, indeed, nothing that led up to his present discomfort.

It is as though he were asleep, anesthetized for a few hours, knocked out, in a prolonged seizure or faint, perhaps in a coma–the only other occasions when we do not remember where we were and what happened around us.

But this person was not in bed asleep or anesthetized with nurses looking after him. He was awake, walking, talking, functioning, interacting with others, doing things. What things? Did he drive somewhere? What did he do there?

Not knowing can be terrifying, the guilt and vulnerability overpowering. And it is worse when he awakens to face a spouse angry over something he said or did, comes out of his blackout in a strange place with someone he does not know in bed beside him, or, God forbid, finds himself cut and bruised with blood splattered on his clothing.

Perhaps the best to be said for blackouts is that the experience is so terrifying, especially for naive drinkers, that some stop drinking or severely restrict consumption.

When a person realizes he has blacked out, the first thing to do is determine the extent of the memory loss. *What is the last thing you remember? Were you home? Did you go out? Alone or with someone? Who? Who else did you see? What did you talk about or do?* Try to reconstruct the pre-blackout part of the evening's drinking.

The purpose of this exercise is to determine whether a true blackout occurred or simply a temporary memory loss, a fade-out.

Hopefully it was the latter. The person has difficulty remembering–everything is hazy, sort of in and out–but he can recall with some help. One man tells of remembering that he got a phone call, but not what was said. Since he was a practicing physician, the situation was a horror for him. Did the phone call relate to a patient? Had he prescribed some medicine or ordered a treatment? His worry was not alleviated until he reached the hospital to look at charts or talk to nurses until he reconstructed what the phone call was about.*

It is embarrassing not to remember and nobody wants to admit it, but at least play detective a little. Look in the fridge to see what was served for dinner. Check your wallet for money or credit card receipts. At least inventory the "dead soldiers." Talk to co-workers, make hints to your spouse. If you can, quiz a couple of sympathetic friends.

Hopefully fragmentary memory will gradually fill out. *Oh yes, I went to the bar and we started on pitchers of beer. Then the party adjourned to Sally's place. Oh God, I didn't really wear that*

*I have collected blackout anecdotes for years. Obviously, in most cases I need to protect the confidentiality of the teller. Nonetheless the stories are true and accurate as reported to me.

lampshade. Even though we'd just met, Sally wouldn't let me drive and brought me home. My car is at her place.

How wonderful to be able to remember. And how fortunate to have such a good friend to see you home safely.

The trouble comes when, try as he will, the person can't remember anything beyond a certain point. It is though a curtain came down. The play went on, but the blacked out person, while present, knows nothing about it. He tries to remember, but can't. No clues help. Even when Sally calls to ask when he's coming for his car, he can't remember. Who's Sally? And where does she live?

Let's leave the hypothetical and look at true life. In the early morning hours of December 31, 1988, Paul Cox, age 21, left a bar near Larchmont, a Westchester County suburb north of New York City. Along with two friends, he got in his car, actually his mother's Chevrolet Impala, and drove off–too fast. Within a quarter mile he approached a curve. Cox heard his friend, Gene Kelly, say, "You're not going to make it."

That is the last thing Cox remembers until the next morning. Around nine o'clock, his mother entered his bedroom and told him the Larchmont police had phoned about 3 a.m. to report her car was abandoned on Fifth Street at Slocum Avenue. She said she checked his room, but he wasn't home. Then she went back to bed. She asked him what happened.

Paul Cox had no idea. So he made up a story about having a flat. When his mother leaves the room, he phones his friend Gene Kelly to ask what happened. Kelly said that Cox missed the curve and hit a guardrail. Kelly said Cox got out of the car and walked off toward home. Kelly and the other friend went back to the bar and drinking.

Cox threw back the covers to discover he was naked. When he got up to dress, he couldn't find the clothes he'd worn. They were new, gifts for Christmas, and he was proud of them. It is of utmost importance to this story that Cox *never did find his clothing*, despite an extensive search.

That night Cox bartended at a New Year's Eve party his parents held for their friends and neighbors. No one noticed anything different about him. There were no scratches, bruises, limps or other signs of injury. But Cox simply couldn't remember the accident, how he got home, or what happened to his clothes–still can't.

By January 2, 1989, all of Larchmont, indeed the whole New York area, was agog over the brutal murders of Drs. Rao and Shanta Chervu, natives of India and prominent physicians. They were found in their bed in their home, stabbed a total of 24 times with a large knife. The room was a sea of blood.

The Chervu murders were of particular interest to Paul Cox and his family, because the Coxes had once lived in that house. Paul had spent his childhood until age seven there, when the dwelling was sold to the Chervus. Indeed, the murders had occurred in his old bedroom. The Coxes devoured news of the murders in newspapers and telecasts.

The Larchmont Police had a difficult time with the murders. There were few clues to work with. About all they knew for certain was that even though the murders were not discovered until Monday, January 2, they occurred in the wee hours of Saturday, December 31, 1988.

This is precisely when Paul Cox was in his blackout, unable to remember or account for several hours of his young life. Could he have possibly, somehow, have committed these ghastly murders and not remember it? He soon began to dream of entering his old home, walking through it, going upstairs, entering his old bedroom, seeing people lying in bed. At first they were faceless. Eventually the people in his dream became his parents. Paul Cox became increasingly upset. Could he have slain the Chervus, thinking he was killing his own parents?

The dreams and worries worsened. Could he have gone to his old home in a blackout and murdered two people? No knife was ever found, nor any bloody clothes. He had awakened naked and never found the clothes he wore. Could he have hidden the knife and attire? If so, where? How could he have gotten home naked? Blacked out, unable to remember, unable to find anyone to help him remember, Cox's worries and fears mounted.

In November 1990, at the urging of his then-girlfriend, Cox joined Alcoholics Anonymous (AA). As part of his recovery program, he began to speak of his fears that he might have murdered the Chervus. This went on for over two years. Then in January 1993, an AA member went to the Larchmont police with Cox's tale.

Detectives discovered that Cox's fingerprints matched those found at the murder scene. On May 20, 1993, Cox was arrested and charged with two counts of intentional murder in the second degree.

Cox went on trial on June 1, 1994. A hung jury resulted and Cox was tried again in October. He was convicted and in March 1995, more than five years after the crime, sentenced to up to a century in prison.

By the time of his conviction, Cox was convinced he had committed the murders–although he had no memory of doing so. His father, Frank Cox, a vice president of Chase Manhattan Bank, believed his son was guilty and rose in court to formally apologize to the children of the murder victims for what his son had done. Cox's lawyer believed his client was a murderer, and chose to argue a defense strategy of temporary insanity. The police, prosecutor and judge certainly considered Cox guilty.

The only people to have trouble believing it were jurors. Two different panels deliberated a total of 15 days and never could find him a double murderer—even though he had confessed to the crimes. He was found guilty of manslaughter. The judge made the decision moot by sentencing Cox to the maximum term, 16 and a half to 50 years on each count—to be served consecutively.

Perhaps Cox did murder those two people. I don't know. But certain it is that no one associated with the case, not Cox, not his parents, not his defense lawyer, certainly not the judge and jury, knew very much about blackouts. There was hardly any testimony about blackouts and none at all reflecting current knowledge.

If they had known the role of memory and consciousness during a blackout, they would have realized it would be extremely unlikely for a person in a blackout to have committed these murders.

Let's leave it right there for now. We will return to the Cox case shortly to discover what it tells us about police procedures and the law relating to blackouts. But first, to understand what happened to Paul Cox, Kevin Price and myriads of others suffering blackouts, we need to consider another remarkable case of memory loss.

3

Life In The Perpetual Present

Much of what we know about human memory and how it works is due to a single, remarkable individual who graduated from high school only with difficulty and has never held a job for long.

H. M., as he is known (the H. stands for Henry and I want to dignify him by using it) is a man in his mid-70s, in good physical health for his age and living in a nursing home. Ordinarily a placid, agreeable person, Henry became depressed one day and complained about "having not done anything with his life." Those around him at once assured him he had done a great deal with his life and was a most important person.

Indeed he is. In their book *From Conditioning to Conscious Recollection: Memory Systems of the Brain,* Psychologists Howard Eichenbaum and Neal J. Cohen describe Henry as "probably the most examined and best known neurological patient ever studied." In his person, Henry has probably done more to advance our knowledge of human memory than any scientist who ever lived.

The story begins in 1933 when Henry, a boy of seven, was knocked down by a bicycle. He hit his head and was unconscious for five minutes. Three years after that accident Henry began to have minor epileptic seizures. His first major seizure occurred on his 16th birthday when he was riding in his parent's car. The seizures continued, making it difficult for Henry to study, but he did graduate from high school in 1947 at age 21. His was a "general" diploma with emphasis on "practical" courses.

Henry worked for a while on an assembly line as a motor winder, but his seizures became more frequent, on the order of 10 minor attacks each day and a major attack each week. He had to give up the job. Large doses of anti-convulsion drugs failed to control the epilepsy, so doctors decided to perform an experimental operation in hopes of ameliorating his devastating seizures.

In 1953, when Henry was 27, surgeon William Scoville performed what is known as a "bilateral medial temporal lobe resection." Lifting up the frontal lobes, he inserted a straw and sucked out an area deep in the brain, which included about two-thirds of Henry's hippocampus on both sides, as well as surrounding tissue. No one knew the function of the hippocampus. Everyone was about to learn.

The operation was a success in that Henry's seizures receded so they could be controlled with drugs.

But there were problems. Immediately after his operation he could not recognize the hospital or the doctors and nurses who took care of him. Even after 17 days in the hospital, he could not find the bathroom. And he recalled nothing of the daily events during his recovery. When he returned home, Henry could not learn the locations of common objects, such as a lawn mower he had used the day before. He did the same jigsaw puzzles and read the same magazines day after day without becoming familiar with them.

Henry lived with his parents, doing household chores, watching TV and solving crossword puzzles. But his mother, who looked after Henry until she was 95, said he was more difficult to care for than a child. At least a child can remember what he's seen or heard. A child can develop a routine. Each day was novel to Henry. "What are we going to do today?" was a question Henry could not answer.

He could not remember to eat or drink or go to bed. If she sent him to the store two blocks away, he could not find his way back home and would just wander off. If she were not present, he would let strangers in and entertain them. He didn't know who they were, but he figured if they came to the door they must be friends.

Following his father's death, Henry attended a rehabilitation workshop and became something of a handyman, performing repetitive tasks. But if he were interrupted, say to go to the bathroom, he could not find his workplace, despite its being marked with a flag. He saw the flag but had no idea what it meant. He had to be shown again the task he was to do.

Eventually his mother and another relative could no longer care for him and he moved into a board and care home where he still resides. He participates in the social activities of the home, watches TV and solves difficult crossword puzzles.

Henry is highly amiable and cooperative, rarely complaining. He has to be quizzed to identify minor problems such as a headache. He never asks for food or drink or to go to bed, but he readily follows directions for all his daily activities. He is aware of his memory disorder but is not especially concerned about it. If given a rather difficult memory question, he may reply, "You know I have a memory problem."

Starting in 1957, Henry was questioned and tested by a succession of psychologists, neurologists and other scientists. Henry endured it with unending good humor–perhaps because he couldn't remember the test or the tester more than a few minutes.

Everything was forever new to him.

The initial aim of the studies was to see to it that the same experimental operation was never performed on another human being. Then, as the testing proceeded, it became clear that Henry offered a unique opportunity to understand memory and how it works in the human brain.

Henry is not without memory. He has much of his procedural and pre-op declarative memory. He can remember his parents, much of his childhood, language, vocabulary, information and skills learned in his youth, and public events and personages through the 1940s. He cannot remember graduating from high school in 1947, however. His recognition of events and personages after 1950 is poor at best. He has no memory of anything after the surgery in 1953.

Henry has immediate memory. If he is not distracted, he will remember a face, name or fact for a short period of time. In his book, *Memory's Ghost,* author Philip J. Hilts reports that Henry's immediate memory lasts about 20 seconds if he is not distracted. On one occasion Henry remembered the number 584 for 15 minutes by keeping it constantly before his attention.

If you were introduced to him, he would have forgotten in as little as 20 seconds not only your name but ever having met you. If someone spoke to him or he was distracted, you wouldn't stay in his memory even that long.

What the surgeon sucked out of Henry's brain was most of his ability to form new memory. This is so debilitating it is hard to even imagine what it might be like.

Henry has no concept of time. He does not know the year, day or minute. He can only guess his age or when an event occurred. He has no sense of elapsed time. Because of his 20 second attention span, it is believed that time speeds up for Henry. An hour is like three minutes to him, a year three hours. About a week has passed since the operation that debilitated him.

His distortion of time gives rise to the question of what Henry sees when he looks in a mirror? Does he remember seeing this person before? Does he recognize himself? He has made a reference to the person in the mirror being older. This suggests that he does recognize himself, but only after looking at his reflection thousands of times over a half century. For Henry to learn is painfully slow and extremely repetitive.

Always amiable, always wanting to please, Henry greets newcomers with the stories about his parents and grandparents. His father came from the south. His grandfather was a sheriff and lived with a bullet close to his heart. That's fine, but the stories are always exactly the same, word for word, and repeated each time he meets someone new–and that can be someone he just met a minute ago.

Tales of Henry's disability are legion. Howard Eichenbaum recalls his first encounter with Henry while driving him from the nursing home to MIT for testing. It was 1980 and Henry was 47 years old. Eichenbaum had stopped at a nearby McDonald's for lunch and left a coffee cup on the dash.

Sitting in the back seat, Henry noticed the coffee cup and said, "Hey, I knew a fellow named John McDonald when I was a boy." He then told some stories about his friend. Eichenbaum writes that he was "impressed" with Henry's elaborate memories of his childhood. The story ended and Henry looked out the window at the passing scenery for a while. When he looked back toward the front he said, "Hey, I knew a fellow named John McDonald when I was a boy." He repeated essentially the same anecdotes, after which he again viewed the scenery. Then he again saw the cup, made the same statement and told the same stories. Repetition ended only when Eichenbaum hid the cup under the car seat. In other words, Henry could recall old memories, but not remember the recall.

On another occasion investigators were driving Henry in a downpour, when the car ahead of theirs spun off the road and crashed. Henry's driver got out to help the victims, becoming drenched. Later the trip continued. The driver complained about being wet and asked Henry if he knew why he was wet. Henry thought a moment and replied, "You were out in the rain...asking directions."

Henry lives in a perpetual present. He cannot find his way back to any place he lived after 1950. He cannot remember any new fact. Information won't stay in his head long enough to be learned.

Eichenbaum and Cohen report that Henry has retained some information to which "he has been exposed excessively." He realizes his parents are now dead. He learned the meaning of a few words, such as astronaut that have come into use since his operation. He knows who Elvis Presley and John Kennedy were, but, as Eichenbaum reports, his memories for these and other facts are "fragmentary and confused at best." To illustrate, Eichenbaum reproduced the following interview between Henry and neuropsychologist Jennie Ogden:

J.O.: Do you know who Elvis Presley is?
Henry: He was a recording star, and he used to sing a lot.
J.O.: Do you think he is still alive, Elvis Presley?
Henry: No, I don't think so.
J.O.: Have you any idea what happened to him?
Henry: Well, I believe he got the first bullet I think was for Kennedy, I think it was.
J.O.: You remember Kennedy?
Henry: Yes, Robert.
J.O.: What was he?
Henry: Well, he was President, I think about three times. He

was appointed President too.
J.O.: He got a bullet. What was that all about?
Henry: Well, they were trying to assassinate him.
J.O.: And did they? Did they kill him or not?
Henry: No, they didn't.
J.O.: So, is he still alive?
Henry: Yes, he is alive, but he got out of politics in a way.
J.O.: I don't blame him.
Henry: No, guess not.
J.O.: How long ago was he the President do you think?
Henry: He became President after Roosevelt. 'Course there was Teddy Roosevelt. That was a long time before that.
J O.: What is Franklin Roosevelt's wife's name?
Henry: I can't think of it.
J.O.: It starts with "E" I think–Eleanor. You were going to say that?
Henry: No I wasn't. I was going to say "Ethel."
Eichenbaum then adds:
"Ethel is the name of Robert Kennedy's widow. Clearly Henry has learned and retained a few of the most famous names of the 1960s. But his knowledge about the details of their notoriety is minimal compared to contemporaries who were saturated with information about them. Furthermore, the information that is retained is disorganized, so that he confuses the individuals and the facts about them. Also, his islands of spared memory contrast with equally impressive failures. For example, despite watching the television news every night in the summer of 1973, he could not identify Watergate or John Dean, although he could guess whom the president was (Nixon) when prompted by the letter N. In 1980 he remembered correctly that a very popular TV situation comedy character Archie Bunker called his son-in-law 'meathead' but incorrectly stated that Howard Cosell did news on television

(he was a sports-caster), and that Barbara Walters was a singer (she is a television journalist)."

Another anecdote reports that a researcher hid a pin in his hand while saying goodbye and shaking hands with Henry–the prick causing him minor pain. The next day Henry did not remember ever meeting the researcher, but he refused to shake hands with him. Yes, some learning occurs with Henry, but it bears little resemblance to what is considered normal.

What must it be like to live in the perpetual present? Henry described it this way: "At the moment everything looks clear to me, but what happened just before? That's what worries me. It's like waking from a dream, I just don't remember." He worries constantly that he may have said or done the wrong thing and asks a dozen times a day, "What did I say?"

In the movie *Memento*, nominated for a 2002 Oscar for best screenplay by Christopher Nolan, an attempt was made to portray a man who had lost his ability to form memory. To get back to his motel or to remember significant people, the protagonist took Polaroid photos on which he wrote names or important information. In a bizarre touch, he had truly vital information tattooed on his body. There are a couple of minor errors, but the movie is gripping and well acted. However I doubt if a person without memory formation could function in society very long. Henry certainly can't.

In the movie, the protagonist lost his memory when a blow to the head destroyed the hippocampus in his brain. The hippocampus is an area about the size of one's little finger and curved into an open C-shape. Early observers thought it resembled a seahorse, hence its name, hippocampus, from the Greek word for sea creature. There are two of them, one on each side of the brain. But in this book I will use the singular hippocampus to refer to both organs.

It lies inside the temporal lobe near the midline, almost in the center of the brain. Recall the surgeon had to lift the frontal lobes of Henry's brain to reach the hippocampus. Having a head injury destroy the hippocampus, as in the movie, is hard to believe, although theoretically possible. On the other hand, there is a case of memory loss similar to Henry's when only a tiny portion of the hippocampus was removed.

When Henry lost his hippocampus he lost his ability to form memory. Clearly, therefore, the organ plays a crucial role in formation of memory. As investigators learned from Henry, loss of the hippocampal function does not affect long-term stored memory, existing procedural, semantic or episodic memory. Henry was a reasonably well-functioning individual, except for the ability to form new memory. His ability to learn and function was gravely restricted.

Aside from surgery and possibly a severe blow to the head, *there is another way to incapacitate the hippocampus. Just start swilling alcohol at a rapid rate on an empty stomach while in a state of fatigue.* In some manner not yet fully understood, the alcohol keeps the hippocampus from receiving chemical signals necessary for memory formation. Anesthetics block memory in a similar fashion, though under controlled surgical conditions.

To understand Kevin Price, Paul Cox and all others in a blackout, one must realize that for the minutes, hours or days they are unconscious in a blackout, they may be thought of as temporary Henry M.s.

The major differences are that Henry is recognized and studied as a person unable to form memory; he is institutionalized, cared for and protected by others; he is not walking the streets, driving a car, hopping into taxis and airplanes; he is not going to a job, say as a surgeon or airline pilot; he does not have access to knives, guns and other dangerous weapons; he is not held legally responsible for his actions by law enforcement and the courts.

4

"Did Anyone Get Anything To Eat?"

Most blackouts do not result in double murders or the deaths of five people in car crashes–Thank God! There are a couple of reasons for this.

First, people who drink to excess often pass out, that is, fall asleep in a drunken stupor. They are recognized as unconscious, in contrast to the blacked out individuals, who still function even if they don't know what they're doing. Second, drinking is usually a social activity, done amid family and friends. Companions may not recognize the blackout, but they know he's had a lot to drink and see that he gets home safely.

Rather than accidents and murders, a perhaps more common experience was related by a suburban couple invited to dinner at a friend's house. It was a typical affair, cocktails followed by a savory dinner, then an evening of conversation and games. The hostess, bright and witty, served an elegant dinner she had prepared and played games expertly. All had a good time. The next day the two couples ran into each other. While exclaiming over the fun of the evening before, the hostess said, "Did anyone get anything to eat?"

Sometime during cocktails she had blacked out and formed no memory of dinner or subsequent events. Her friends were surprised because she had acted normally, except for being somewhat "high." She did not act drunk or say or do anything the least improper.

There must be something about hosting a party that encourages blackouts. Dennis Wholey, writing in his book *The Courage to Change*, reports, "Blackouts were common to me for many years. I once threw a party for five hundred people in New York City. To this day, I can remember only one person who was there."

How common our housewife's experience is may never be known. She may have thought her failure to remember ordinary. And nothing untoward happened. She was safe in her own home. She did not drive anywhere, endanger herself or anyone, or get into an argument.

Even if the blackout did worry her, perhaps as a symptom of a "drinking problem," she was unlikely to speak of it, even to her husband or friends. Not getting drunk, being able to "control one's liquor" are socially desirable in society. Even the most besotted try to pretend they are not drunk. Actors are taught to portray drunks as trying to appear sober.

It is unlikely our suburban hostess and others like her would admit to others they blacked out. Rather than admit to the problem, it is easier to privately swear not to let it happen again.

Hopefully it doesn't. But one must wonder how many crimes, misdemeanors, traffic accidents, quarrels, domestic violence, divorces, bar fights, lost friendships, wasted opportunities and unemployment are caused by actions taken and words said during a blackout. And if the person blacked out cannot remember what happened, he cannot even apologize. Nor can the offended person realize the blacked out person did not know what she was doing.

Alcoholics Anonymous literature from the 1940s reports this man's experience:

"Every time I blacked out, and that was every time I drank, there was always that gnawing fear, 'what did I do this time?' Once I found out. Many alcoholics have learned they can bring their bottle to a cheap movie theater and drink, sleep, wake up and drink again in the darkness. I had repaired to one of these one morning with my jug, and when I left late in the afternoon, I picked up a newspaper on the way home. Imagine my surprise when I read in a page-one 'box' that I had been taken from the theater unconscious around noon that day, removed by ambulance to a hospital and stomach-pumped, and then released. Evidently I had gone right back to the movie with a bottle, stayed there several hours, and started home with no recollection of what had happened."

In his book, *The Courage to Change,* Dennis Wholey includes this passage written by Gary Crosby, eldest son of Bing and Dixie Lee Crosby: "Sometimes...I would have a three-day-and-three night blackout, when I'd just be gone. I'd wind up in some other town, in bed with somebody I had never seen before, in a room I had never been in before. I would have to go over to the desk, pull out the Gideon Bible, and see the name of the hotel and the town stamped on it. I couldn't just call downstairs and ask, 'Where am I?'"

Consider this description written by comedian Shecky Greene in the same book: "After these binges, there was bad depression. I couldn't face anybody later on because I didn't know what I'd done. I was having a tremendous number of blackouts–just about every time I drank. I drank until I had a blackout. Lots of times near the end I would see somebody after a drinking session and I'd say, 'Hi, Charlie, how are you?' And he'd say, 'you got the guts to talk to me, after what you did, you dirty rat? You used to be a nice guy.' Then I would get into saying, 'What did I do?' I would come back into the hotel and somebody else would say, 'Boy, did you tie one on last night. You know what you did? You tore the telephone out of the wall.' I had a thing about telephones. I went around tearing telephones out of walls."

Dr. Donald Goodwin, one of the few scholars to do serious study of blackouts, reported this case: "A 39-year-old salesman awoke in a strange hotel room. He had a mild hangover but otherwise felt normal. His clothes were hanging in the closet; he was clean-shaven. He dressed and went down to the lobby. He learned from the clerk that he was in Las Vegas and that he had checked in two days previously. It had been obvious that he had been drinking, the clerk said, but he hadn't seemed very drunk.

"The date was Saturday the 14th. His last recollection was of sitting in a St. Louis bar on Monday the 9th. He had been drinking all day and was drunk, but could remember everything perfectly until about 3 p.m. when 'like a curtain dropping,' his memory went blank. It remained blank for approximately five days. Three years later, it was still blank. He was so frightened by the experience that he abstained from alcohol for two years."

Another author identified as Chuck "C," writing in the book *A New Pair of Glasses,* says he also gave up drinking following a *four week blackout,* from Christmas 1945 to some time after the middle of January 1946.

How common is the alcohol blackout? How much of a problem do we have here?

If it is true that seven or eight per cent of the adult population of the United States are alcoholics, then it may be said the incidence of blackouts among them is close to 100 per cent, whether they know it or not. Many in prisons arrived there because of acts committed while in blackouts. Incidence may be common among the homeless.

Professor Aaron M. White of the Duke University Medical Center reports a study of 13,000 men and women in the general population. Roughly 15 per cent reported having blackouts. In a similar study of 230 men, one-quarter reported blackouts. A study of 2,076 Finnish men reported 35 per cent had at least one blackout during the previous year.

Because fatigue and rapid consumption, as in binges, may cause blackouts, they are believed to be epidemic on college campuses.

One former student recalls playing a game called "Superbowl" during his university days. The aim of the game was to earn "first downs" by swilling different drinks in 10 different rooms. thus scoring a "touchdown." "Extra points" were earned in some fashion. This particular individual woke up, Band-aids up and down his arms, remembering nothing. He was later told he had won the game by scoring four touchdowns. Fortunately, the blackout so terrified him, he gave up his "football" career.

Several studies indicate almost 25 per cent of students who consume alcohol have blackouts. Professor White reports his own studies showing females at greater risk of blackouts than males.

Substantial evidence suggests that even naïve drinkers are at risk of blackouts. Better said, a blackout can occur to anyone at anytime they drink to excess. A woman of my acquaintance considers herself a light drinker, consuming a glass of wine or cocktail during an evening–except on one occasion. She and her girlfriends started downing dry martinis. That much my friend remembers. What she doesn't remember is going bowling, where she apparently scored her average, or getting home. Nor does she have memory to this day of dropping a bowling ball on her friend's toe, breaking it.

Few statistics exist on how many or how often social drinkers and weekend imbibers suffer blackouts, that is, periods when they cannot remember what happened. One study suggests the incidence of blackouts may be 30 to 40 per cent among this group, but that does not suggest how often they occur.

There are reports of pilots flying cross-country and surgeons performing operations while blacked out. Perhaps better evidence of the pervasiveness of blackouts may be found on the Internet. Call up "alcohol blackout" at Yahoo.com and it lists 10,010 items on the subject.

But, in truth, no one really knows how often blackouts occur, and that is the measure of the problem. We don't know because we haven't yet learned to recognize when a person has blacked out. We can't study him while he's in that state. We have to wait until he comes out of it and can tell us he can't remember what happened for a period of time.

Blackouts may be the most common neurological dysfunction known to man, occurring for thousands of years, but they remain virtually unstudied. In the late 1960s and early 1970s, hospitalized alcoholics were questioned about blackouts. Others were given large amounts of spirits to drink, then tested to see if they blacked out. Some did.

This research was useful and we will look at it shortly. The point here is that three-decade-old research is still being cited as up-to-date information. And it isn't. Brain researchers, working with both humans and animals and using MRIs and PET scans, increasingly zero in on what human memory is, how it works and how it may be interfered with. It is of great significance that the studies of Henry M. began just about the time research into blackouts was abandoned. Our ignorance of a common and potentially dangerous condition is immense.

A major thesis of this book, the rationale for the work that has gone into it, is an appeal for scientific study of blackouts to be resumed. Now that we know the blacked out person is not forgetting or malingering, but not forming memory, it becomes possible to identify and study him.

In Chapter Nine I will propose a simple memory test that may identify the blacked out person so research can be resumed. The test will certainly be useful to spouses, police, bartenders, hospital workers who must deal with the mindless and unconscious person in a blackout.

Despite the lack of study, it is possible to cite some of the characteristics of blackouts. Let's begin with those.

1. **There are at least three types of memory disturbances** associated with alcohol. In the pass out, the drinker falls asleep in an alcoholic stupor. He cannot remember because he was asleep. In the fade out, the person, cannot remember parts of what happened the day or night before. His memory is said to fade in and out. But he will remember in time, when he is reminded of what happened. In the true blackout, the drinker walks, talks, does various things, but he has absolutely no memory of it and never will.

2. **Blackouts are unpredictable.** No one, including the drinker, knows when or if they will occur. If a person, for some nonsensical reason, set out to have a blackout, chances are he would pass out or become exceedingly drunk and suffer a terrible hangover.

3. **Not everyone has blackouts.** Some long-time, heavy drinkers claim to have never blacked out. Chances are that if they keep at it long enough they will.

4. **Some drinkers are highly susceptible to blackouts,** experiencing them often, even every time they drink. No one knows the neurological effects of repeated blackouts.

5. **Some people don't know they have blacked out.** The episode was of short duration or nothing unusual happened. Maybe they were alone. Another way to describe it might be that the

person went away for a while and was not missed by others–or himself.

6. **It is not easy to recognize when a person has blacked out.** He or she appears intoxicated, perhaps, but they talk (usually a form of banter) and act with no indication their memory is gone. I believe there are ways to identify a blacked out person. And it can be important to do so.

7. **Food consumption and certain medicines may affect** whether a blackout occurs. Fatigue and lack of sleep may also be a factor.

8. **The duration of blackouts varies** from a few minutes to a few hours to several days in extreme cases. When the person "awakens," usually from sleep the next morning, the only change is loss of memory, unless he has cuts and bruises from a fight or accident. There are reported cases, however, of people coming out of blackouts while still functioning and not asleep.

9. **Blackouts occur to moderate and even first-time drinkers,** although more frequently among alcoholics. Having a blackout is not *per se* a symptom of alcoholism, although it is usually listed among them.

10. **Blackouts can be prevented.** Despite their unpredictability, there are indications that such factors as fatigue, food consumption and how fast a person drinks may have more to do with blackouts than how much a person drinks. People with a history of memory disturbances while drinking should learn to avoid or at least pace their drinking.

11. **Aloneness plays an important role** in the consequences of blackouts. If Kevin Price had not driven off by himself, if his girlfriend, any conscious person had been with him–even if that person had been quite inebriated–he or she could have asked him where he was going and kept him from turning around on the parkway. The blacked out person does not have the judgment

and cognitive skills to ask for help and may well end up lost, alone and in peril.

5
Ether's First Cousin

Imagine for a moment that a new disease has struck planet Earth. It attacks various organs of the human body, but most especially the brain, greatly impairing judgment and cognition. The greatest damage seems to occur in the hippocampal area, leaving the victim in a zombie-like state, his ability to form memory gone. Because of this the disease is popularly known as "Blackout."

People all over the world, including Antarctica, are afflicted. Victims number in the millions. The attacks occur on repetitive bases, sometimes even daily, resulting in accidents, crimes and other forms of violence. The cost of the disease is said to run into the billions of dollars, not counting lost wages or the toll on marriage and family life.

Imagine also that leaders all over the world have declared Blackout a public health emergency and called for international accords to halt spread of the disease. The United Nations meets in special session. The President of the United States, addressing a joint session of Congress on prime time, unveils an 11-point program to combat the disease. He calls for a War on Blackout and asks for billions in research and to assist victims and their families. Committees of Congress hold hearings on the problems Blackout creates for the nation's legal system.

CNN, Fox News, MSNBC surrender their entire schedules to news of the War on Blackout, concentrating on the human side of the outbreak. Their interviews with the shaking, slurring victims are truly pathetic, their questioning of distraught wives and tearful children heart rending. Money pours into the Red Cross and other charities to aid the victims and their families.

Universities and pharmaceutical houses drop other research to concentrate on Blackout. Aim is to find some means of early detection, leading perhaps to a preventative vaccine. The Center for Disease Control (CDC) is the first to offer hope, pointing out that attacks of the disease seem to last only a few hours, days at the most, then they go into remission for a period of time. Long-term effects of Blackout are not yet known. The CDC alerted physicians that small quantities of ethanol seemed to alleviate some of the shaking and other symptoms following attacks of Blackout.

So much for imagination. The reality of blackouts is that none of the above has happened. The only serious research into blackouts was done over 30 years ago. Further study has been isolated and sporadic.

No one has studied the words and actions of a person in a blackout to try to determine what's going on in his mind. Indeed, such is the depth of our neglect, no research has been done to try to detect when a person has blacked out. No one knows and no one is trying to find out.

And the one in a blackout is the last person ever to be able to tell us.

So, there is an impasse of ignorance. The person in a blackout, one of the more common neurological dysfunctions known to man, remains a medical mystery.

In even trying to discuss the blackout, I tread on unexplored terrain; filled with quicksand I am sure. But somebody has to step into the unknown sooner or later.

Let's begin by looking at alcohol, the offending substance. Alcohol is a simple compound, occurring naturally in nature. It is formed from carbon, hydrogen and oxygen, the building blocks of life (C_2H_5OH). Everything from potatoes to coconuts can be made into alcohol in its ethanol form.

The ancient Egyptians relaxed with beer and wine after a hard day of pyramid building. Before them the Sumerians enjoyed beer. It is reasonable to assume the Cro Magnons and Neanderthals sat in their caves enjoying the fruits of fermentation and wondering why they couldn't remember the last couple of days. Perhaps chimps and gorillas may develop a taste for rotten fruit.

During all this time, the grape and the grain have been praised by poets and cursed by the overindulgent, lauded, lamented, laughed at and illegalized. The history of the world could almost be written in terms of a single substance, its uses and abuses.

Alcohol is all things to all people. Said a better way, alcohol may well affect every person differently. The problem in controlling alcohol abuse is not just what the drug does to the person, but what the person does to the drug. Is the drinker male or female? How old? How heavy in weight? Has she eaten and how long ago? What is her emotional state? When did she last sleep and how well?

The effects of alcohol vary with the individual–and they vary each time she consumes. One drink may make a person relaxed and mellow. Another individual (or the same individual another time) may become euphoric and stimulated. A third may become drowsy, perhaps a little dizzy, and want a nap.

But if a person is going to have that first drink–or a second, a tenth–he must understand that ethanol, the kick in that glass or bottle, is one hydrogen ion shy of being the drug ether. Yes, dimethyl ether, the early anesthetic that made modern surgery possible. Go back even further, and ethanol itself was the anesthetic of choice. Whiskey was dispensed to the Civil War soldier about to have his leg amputated. Many of our modern anesthetics are forms of ether.

Whatever else it may be, alcohol is a depressant, sedative and anesthetic. Drink enough of it and you become unconscious, either the blacked out variety or the passed out. Drink still more and rapidly enough and you may die from alcoholic poisoning. It happens occasionally.

Alcohol a depressant? Can this be true? What about the celebrated alcoholic "high," when the person feels bright, mentally sharp, confident, full of laughter, euphoria and well-being? The writer has never written better, the actor never more in command of his role, the hostess more beautiful and witty, the bachelor more charming, his prey more appealing.

Perhaps, but many a writer, actor, architect, etc. has admitted the work he once thought so fantastic while drinking was quite inferior when sober. And the glamorous maiden or the dashing swain often seems less so by light of a sober morning.

Anyone can test it. Just don't drink at a cocktail party some time. The conversation may be bright and witty, but it is also disjointed. Thoughts and ideas aren't developed and the unwritten rules of conversation are ignored. It is more banter than conversation.

But the high is fun for the drinker. Trouble is it doesn't last long, try as a person will to maintain it. Whether in a few minutes or hours or the next morning, the high is followed by a let down that's truly depressing. Of course a little hair of the dog helps sometimes.

The high occurs because one of the first effects of alcohol is to suppress inhibition. The bars to thought and action, the restraints to expression are lowered. She feels relaxed, confident, able to express thoughts and perform action like never before, fearless. The individual she just met, glass in hand, seems so likable, a real friend. She's never had so much fun, laughed so hard or felt so beautiful. Yes, life is wonderful.

I submit that the alcoholic high–and the vain search for its maintenance–is why people drink in the first place. It certainly isn't because they like the taste of drink. A beer or highball on a hot day can be refreshing, but so is water or juice. Beer and wine taste sour, musty and turned. Children spit it out or gag. A taste for most forms of ethanol must be developed.

True, some drink to reach oblivion. They want to get drunk. The fellow sidling up to the bar and ordering doubles is a staple of movies about jilted lovers. One man tells of mailing his car keys back to himself then checking into a hotel with his supply of booze, turning on the TV and (apparently) happily drinking himself mindless. I hope this was only an occasional event, because drinking to get drunk, at least on a regular basis, is an indicator of addiction and alcoholism. His device of mailing his keys home may keep his vehicle from damage, but if he drinks himself into a blackout, he can still take a cab or hop a plane.

No drinker cares about what booze does to the stomach, liver, kidney, blood stream. That first glass is lifted to create the desired effect on the brain. There is no other reason to drink.

At the moment pharmaceutical houses in the U.S. and Europe are working hard, making huge investments, to develop a drug to inhibit alcohol's effect on the brain. In other words, a person could drink and not feel its effects. At first glance this seems foolishness. Who on earth would want to? But it should be said such a drug, were it to be developed, might promote the responsible use of alcohol. And that is everyone's goal, the holy use of the grail.

6

"What's A Blackout?"

Let's now lift that first glass. Why not? It's five o'clock; the day's work is done. Relax a little. Maybe it's TGIF and the whole weekend lies ahead. A good time to party. So our friend stops at a bar or maybe drops in at a cocktail party. It's cocktail hour, isn't it?

What's important in this scenario is the time. Five o'clock, maybe later. Lunch was hours ago. So, when our friend lifts a glass, perhaps a highball or martini, he is swallowing significant amounts of alcohol into an empty stomach.

What happens next? Ethanol is a very simple compound and can be absorbed quickly, a matter of minutes. Some passes through the stomach walls and reaches the bloodstream almost immediately. More of the alcohol exits the stomach to the small intestine, the duodenum, where it is rapidly absorbed into the bloodstream from there.

How long does that take? Not very long. If our friend last ate at midday, chances are the alcohol is in his bloodstream before he says, "I'll have another drink, bartender."

On an empty stomach alcohol virtually streaks into the bloodstream. The only way for the drug to go into effect quicker would be to inject it into a blood vessel.

Rule No. 1: *If a person wants to have a blackout or get drunk and pass out, the quickest way is to drink on an empty stomach. If the person wants to drink, have fun, stay reasonably sober, then by all means consume food before and while drinking.*

If our friend had a late lunch or snacked in mid-afternoon, better yet, if he had a full meal of meat and potatoes before sidling up to the bar, then his chances of a blackout are reduced. It takes awhile for the stomach to break down food, especially complex proteins and starches. A sort of slurry is created in the stomach and this then passes to the duodenum. When alcohol is added to the slurry, it is still absorbed–but at a much slower rate.

Our friend will still get just as high or drunk as he would have on an empty stomach. It will simply take him longer to do so. This was observed long before science figured out how it works. In many cultures, such as Spain, food is always consumed along with alcoholic beverages. In the U.S. numerous states require that any establishment serving alcohol must also serve food. Conversely, some states forbid the serving of food such as peanuts, pretzels or popcorn from communal dishes for health reasons, not realizing such rules encourage drunkenness. Inebriation is a far greater menace than a few germs from the nut bowl.

Once the alcohol enters the bloodstream it is rapidly distributed throughout the body and gains access to all tissues, including the fetus in pregnant women. A woman drunk while pregnant is carrying a drunken child.

Alcohol is soluble in fat, so it has a greater affinity for fatty tissue. This may afford a slight advantage to overweight people in drinking contests.

The foremost organ to be affected by alcohol is the brain, which is 50 per cent fat.

How long is the alcohol going to remain there? The body has a mechanism for ridding itself of alcohol. A small amount can be excreted via the lungs. The odor of the breath is not a reliable indicator of alcohol consumption, since it comes, not from alcohol vapors, but from impurities in the alcoholic beverages.

The belief persists that pure alcohol in the form of vodka does not smell on the breath. It does of course. I knew one teacher who tried to mask the odor of alcohol with orange juice. His students said he smelled like a screwdriver. (For the teetotaler, that's a cocktail made from vodka and orange juice, not a tool.)

Upon entering the bloodstream, the alcohol goes to the liver where a small amount is metabolized on the first pass-through. Eventually ADH (alcohol dehydrogenase) converts the alcohol to acetaldehyde. This is then converted to water and carbon dioxide by the actions of ALDH (acetaldehyde dehydrogenase). (The drug antabuse blocks the actions of ALDH and acetaldehyde builds up, making the person violently ill. Antabuse is occasionally given to alcoholics to keep them from drinking.)

How long does it take to metabolize alcohol? It depends on body weight (and probably liver weight), but it averages approximately one ounce of pure alcohol per three hours in adults. Thus, if our friend drinks one ounce of 100 proof whiskey, which is 50 per cent alcohol–most drinks are made "heavier" than that–it will take an hour and a half for the body to get rid of it, three hours if two such drinks are consumed.

As John H. Woodward, Ph.D., wrote in the *Principles of Addictive Medicine,* the "bible" of the field, "...the time for an individual to become sober after even moderate intake of ethanol can be substantial."

The amounts and types of ADH and ALDH vary by gender and ethnic groups. Women generally have less ADH activity than men. This results in significantly higher blood alcohol levels in women, even more than would be expected based solely on differences in weight. Women are simply more vulnerable to the effects of alcohol.

About half the people of Japanese ancestry have a variant in their ALDH that makes them less able to metabolize alcohol. Levels of acetaldehyde in these persons after drinking may be 10 times higher than in those with normal ALDH. Even small amounts of alcohol can produce essentially the same nausea as antabuse. Studies have extended these findings to people of Chinese and Taiwanese ancestry. ALDH variants have not yet been detected in persons of European descent.

These liver enzymes may account for the greater tolerance some individuals have to alcohol, as well as the observed tolerance the children of alcoholics often possess. But all this is in the hypothesis stage at the moment.

Return to our friend, the drinker. The alcohol has now reached the brain–every part of it. No function of the organ is unaffected–inhibitions, physical movement and coordination (motor skills), speech, memory, vision and other senses, thought processes, certainly emotions and above all judgment.

The effects of the alcohol on the brain are imperceptible at first, but become apparent as more is consumed. Our friend gradually loses control of his limbs, speech, actions and thoughts. And the deterioration is in direct relation to how fast he consumes alcohol.

If he continues to drink, flooding the brain with alcohol, it's functions gradually shut down until he inevitably passes out and becomes immobile. That is a life-saving function of the brain.

Where is the blackout in this continuum? When does our friend reach that state and why? To answer, we must ask another question. How do we form memory?

Memory is the mother of all wisdom.
—Aeschylus, Prometheus Unbound

All living creatures, it may be argued, have some sort of memory, if only a little-understood instinct or genetic imprint. Birds, fish, insects, various mammals migrate over long distances, returning to the place of their birth to create a new generation. How they do this remains an enchanting mystery. Dogs and cats traverse long distances to return to home and loved ones. Rats, Pavlov's dogs, even earthworms learn mazes and other complex activities by some type of memory (or programming). Microbes adapt to antibiotics and other drugs designed to kill them and thrive on. And a veteran gardener will insist plants and flowers have feelings.

The above quotation indicates that at least 2,500 years ago the Greeks were cognizant of the role memory plays in making human beings human.

If a blackout is a disturbance of memory, a loss of or inability to form memory, then answering that young man's question leads to a second query: What is memory? Memory enables us to learn, pass on information from one generation to the next, develop a civilization, probe outer space, build a computer to be an artificial memory, and meet our friends and family in a crowded restaurant for lunch. But what is memory and how does it work?

There is a long history of memory studies, which can be summarized with brevity.

In the 1960s, some thought memory was encoded (engrams) and stored in specific molecules of the brain. Attempts were made to "transfer" memory by dissolving the brains of trained rats and injecting them into untrained rats. Some claims of success were made, but the idea was soon abandoned. How could there be enough molecules to represent the infinite variety of our memories?

Another and popular way to view memory is as a warehouse or filing system. Memory is said to be "stored" in particular areas of the brain, then "transferred" to some other areas at another stage. In this scheme, a memory is stored in its own place according to some organizational plan until such time as it is needed, whereupon a search is made to retrieve the item. This makes a certain amount of sense. After all, isn't this the way we store information in books and libraries, appointment calendars, diaries and the hard drive of computers?

Writing in *Principles of Psychology* in 1890, William James wrote: "An object which is recollected...is one which has been absent from consciousness altogether, and now revives anew. It is brought back, recalled, fished up, so to speak, from a reservoir in which, with countless other objects, it lay buried and lost from view."

The problem with the warehouse model was that no one could find the warehouse. Using PET scans, MRIs and other probes, scientists could find no area in the brain given over to memory storage. If there were "filing cabinets" for memory, they were stuck in nooks and crannies all over the place.

Now came the concept of memory as a switchboard. Memory is a set of associations between neural representations interconnected by a switchboard. To recognize my wife from all the other women in that restaurant and all the other women I know sort of lights up a switchboard to make a great many comparisons almost instantly, then connects recognition to the motor and sensory portions of the brain so I walk to the correct table and smile when I see her.

A scientist named K. S. Lashley did in the switchboard (and warehouse) theory almost single-handedly. He trained rats to run a maze, then made cuts in cortical areas of the animals' brains.

Lashley hoped to sever the connections that enabled the rats to run the maze. The rats kept on running. He made more cuts in many directions. The rats continued to run the maze, losing the ability only after a great damage was done to the cortical areas.

I am indebted for this analysis to Psychologists Howard Eichenbaum and Neal J. Cohen in their book *From Conditioning to Conscious Recollection: Memory Systems of the Brain.* They go on to state:

"It's not that these metaphors are totally wrong or useless, but that they are misleading in treating memory as a special category of brain events or brain activities. Instead, we would suggest that memory be conceived of as a fundamental property of brain systems and a natural outcome of the brain's various processing activities, rather than an entity stored in the brain."

Memory is not a place, a part or a process, but a property, that is, a quality, trait or attribute peculiar to the brain as a whole.

Nor is memory just one thing. Remembering the multiplication tables is different than the memory of our first kiss. And neither has much in common with remembering how to ride a bicycle, the year the Spanish Armada was defeated, where we were when the World Trade Center was bombed, the date it happened, the difference in meaning of the words synonym and antonym, or the color of our grandmother's eyes–to name a few.

Memory is extremely complex. It comes in apparently infinite varieties. Some people remember poetry learned in childhood, while others never forget a number. Spatial memory is easy for a few folks, while others never forget a face–or a name. Some lucky individuals have minds like quicksilver, the information they need recalled at will. Others have many "senior moments" (nomenaphasia–cannot speak the name), when they cannot retrieve names they know very well. Words like gizmo, doodad, whosis and whatsis are much used.

It is at least arguable that every person's memory is different in small or greater ways. Our memory may be what makes us distinctive as individuals.

To make some sense of all this complexity, psychologists and neuroscientists speak of two types of memory, *declarative and procedural–knowing as against knowing how.*

Procedural memory allows us to tie our shoe laces, tell time, brush our teeth, ride a bike, drive a car, scramble some eggs, do a back flip and kiss a loved one–among many others. Recall is so swift it is almost automatic.

Procedural memory is seldom forgotten. In blackouts and even total amnesia, procedural memory usually remains intact. Thus procedural memory appears to have its own specialized neural processing system apart from other systems.

Declarative memory has been further subdivided into *episodic and semantic,* with other subdivisions under those. This was stated earlier, but to review: Episodic memory stores past events in a sequential fashion as temporarily dated episodes–that first kiss, graduation, marriage, birth of children, the new job, purchase of first house. Semantic memory stores organized information, concepts, vocabulary and knowledge of the world without regard to time sequencing–all our schooling, job skills, names and locations of friends and family, language, nearly everything we learn and use in a lifetime.

How is memory formed? Over the years, I have seen the answer to that question grow from hypothesis to virtual certainty.

The brain is composed of cells, called neurons. Many of these are specialized, perhaps to form and store memories. Think of a neuron as a shrub or bush. The trunk is the nucleus of the cell and the branches and roots are dendrites and axons. (See Fig. 1) There are billions of these "shrubs" crammed into our craniums, yet none of the branches ever touch one other.

To do anything, such as type these words or remember how to spell them, messages must be sent virtually instantly across millions of neurons. (See Fig. 2) This is done chemically. Neuron A creates a chemical (a neurotransmitter) which spills across the open space between "branches" to bind with (a neuroreceptor) and open a passageway to Neuron B, etc. There are multiple transmitters and billions to trillions of receptors, each with its own purpose in that magical organ called the human brain.

Now, let's simplify a complex process and form a memory. Let's say you want to remember where your car is parked in a large lot. You observe where your car is in relation to the street or exit. Yes, Row B, Space 6.

This information goes at once into immediate memory in the hippocampal area. Next the hippocampal cells release the chemical glutamate, one of the most common neurotransmitters in the brain. The glutamate now forms a vital link with NMDA (N-methyl-D-aspartate) receptors in the hippocampus. The NMDA then opens a calcium channel, which carries an electrical impulse with long-term potential (LTP) to short-

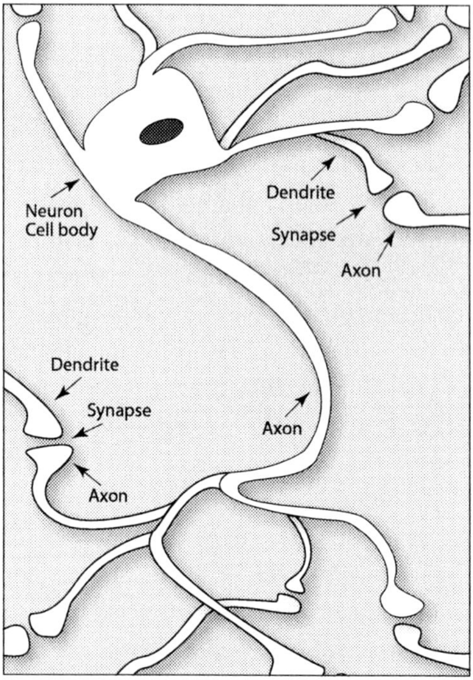

Fig. 1 Schmetic Drawing of Neuron

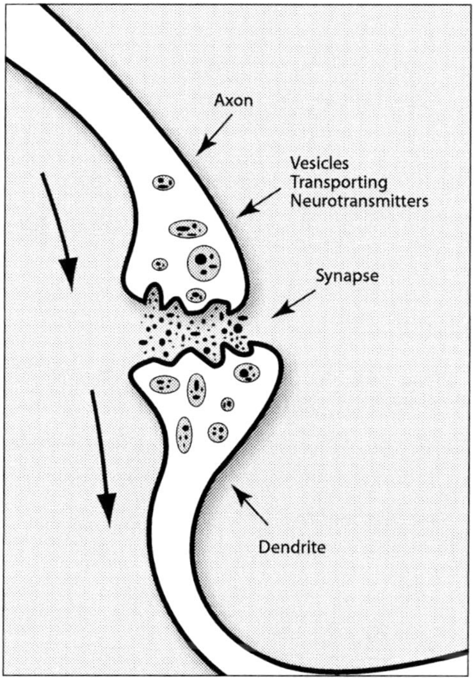

Fig. 2 Normal Dentrite-Axon Communication

term memory.

The information about the location of your car will hopefully remain in short-term memory until you get back to it. Equally hopefully the information will then be discarded or forgotten as no longer important. If not, your mind will become an impossible clutter of useless information.

But suppose this is your first day on a new job and the parking place is to be permanently assigned to you. In some marvelous but unknown way, the brain recognizes the importance of the location and lodges the clues to your parking place in long-term memory (LTM). You do not have to record the location of your car every time you park. Your marvelous memory already tells you Row B, Space 6.

Even better, with continued use the brain will lead you unerringly to your car without thinking about it. You may even forget the clues of Row B, Space 6 and not be able to tell your secretary where your car is so she can fetch the briefcase you left in the vehicle that morning.

"What's a blackout?"

The answer to that young man's question of a decade and a half ago is now at hand. That it seems a simple answer should not belie the immense amount of research, study, thought and time, by many people, that led to it.

Alcohol in sufficient quantities prevents the NMDA *receptors in the hippocampus from reacting to the glutamate neurotransmitter, thus blocking formation of memory.*

Glutamate continues to pour out of the cells, but the excessive alcohol has shut down the NMDA receptors. (See Fig. 3) They are closed and will not open until the body gets rid of the alcohol hours later. Think of a lock and key. Glutamate, the key, keeps turning, but the lock (NMDA) will not open. Another analogy is a lock in a canal. The ship of memory cannot move forward until the lock of NMDA opens.

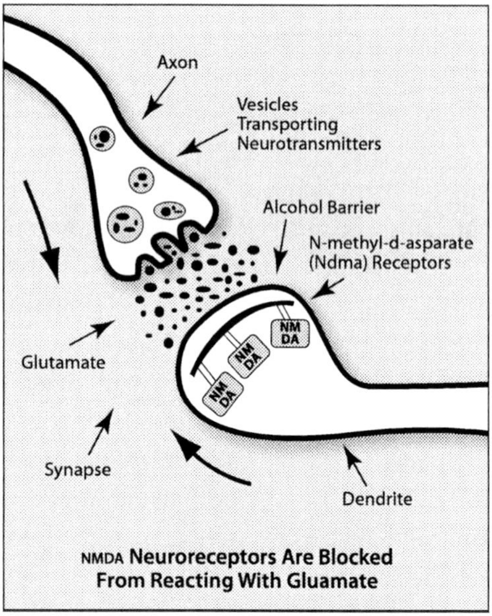

NMDA Neuroreceptors Are Blocked From Reacting With Gluamate

Fig. 3
Alcohol Inhibited Dendrite-Axon Communication

The new observation or fact never leaves immediate memory. No short-term memory or new working memory is formed, nor is memory of any kind. The information in the immediate memory soon withers and disappears, gone forever. The person has blacked out. He is not forming any memory. He is Henry M.–lost, incapable of learning, unable to remember anything or to act upon it.

Like Henry M., the blacked out person's immediate memory is intact, along with recall of his procedural and declarative memory. Without short-term or working memory, he knows how to drive a car but not where he is going. He can walk but has no idea what he is to do when he arrives. He can talk in a superficially rational way for short periods. If distracted or interrupted he will never recall or finish what he was saying. He remembers everything in his long-term memory, all his schooling, language, where he lives, etc., but nothing that happened a minute ago. He will never learn anything new more than momentarily. He will forget even the act of remembering.

And he will never know. Even when the alcohol wears off and the blackout ends, he will never remember what happened while it lasted. Again, no memory was formed. He could have married the stranger lying in bed next to him, run up huge bills on his credit cards, gambled away his life savings, sold his business, killed five people in a head-on crash on the Garden State Parkway, slashed the throats of two people who lived in the house where he formerly resided. He will never remember it.

A blackout is serious, a risk every time it happens.

I have presented here, albeit greatly simplified, what I believe to be the prevailing scientific explanation for the alcohol blackout. But the GABA system may also be involved. GABA (gamma aminobutyric acid) is another neurotransmitter. Where Glutamate is excitatory, GABA is inhibitory. It follows then that if alcohol (the first cousin to ether) intensifies the actions of GABA, it may depress memory formation.

I tend to believe blockage of the NMDA system brings on a blackout, because of the abruptness with which the memory loss occurs. The person is forming memory, then he isn't. The GABA system seems to be affected more gradually, bringing on a period of fuzziness preceding the memory loss. I suspect the GABA system is more likely involved in what I have called the alcoholic fadeout, as well as the loss of memory associated with Halcion, a sleeping pill, and Rohypnol, a date rape drug. These are described in the appendix.

7
Living With Blackouts

Consider the blacked out person. He may exhibit the usual manifestations of over-indulgence. He may be a bit unsteady on his feet, his speech may be slurred, his thoughts repetitive, but his brain still functions–except for one thing. The NMDA receptors in his hippocampus have shut down, and memory of all new events and sensations cannot take place.

How did that happen? Our friend, like Kevin Price, has hit the bottle many times and never blacked out. Why now? Clearly, something different happened this time than on all the other occasions.

The shutdown of NMDA receptors appears to happen abruptly. The brain alcohol level reaches a certain point, and the receptors are blocked–all at once. The person remembers everything up to a certain point, then nothing. It's like hitting a wall barring memory. Kevin Price was in the bathroom of his friend's house. Next he woke up in a hospital room with a broken leg. Paul Cox was warned that he was driving too fast, then woke up in his bed.

Serious study is needed, but the abrupt onslaught of blackouts may explain why they are so unpredictable, occurring one time but not another. It may also offer a way to perhaps prevent the blackout from occurring.

Consider again the person in a blackout. We have tales of pilots flying cross-country and surgeons performing major surgeries while blacked out. In other stories people rent cars, drive long distances, get on and off airplanes, check into hotels, ride in taxis while blacked out.

This can only mean they did not act drunk. They must have appeared reasonably sober or none of the above was likely to happen. Hospitals do not allow surgeons with alcohol on their breath to operate, let alone weaving, stumbling doctors with shaking hands and slurred, nonsensical speech. They would be forcibly removed if they tried.

Nor do airlines allow such people at the controls of an airliner. They do not even allow them on board as passengers. Rent-a-car companies do not lease vehicles to obviously inebriated drivers. Unless it's a flophouse, hotels do not let slobbering, unruly, ready-to-pass-out drunks register for a room, and taxi drivers are notorious for not accepting drunken passengers. Nobody wants the trouble they cause.

The manifestations of drunkenness are universally known, so it must be concluded that these traveling, operating and functioning blacked-out persons did not act any worse than mildly inebriated.

Do we have a clue here? If the blacked-out person does not act particularly inebriated, then perhaps he is simply not as drunk as the person who passes out. Obviously, the person blacks out before he passes out. It is at least possible–and frightening–that an individual could pass the police sobriety test (walking a straight line, touching his nose) while blacked out.

A person in a blackout is difficult to detect.

It is pure theory on my part, but I wonder if the blackout results not so much from consuming great quantities of alcohol, but from drinking too fast and on an empty stomach.

Kevin Price arrived late at the party on the New Jersey shore, then played catch-up, swilling beers rapidly. Others at the party had presumably drunk as many beers or more without blacking out. But they had been partying longer. Paul Cox drank several kamikazes, a very strong vodka cocktail, just prior to his blackout.

Serious research is needed, but it is at least possible that a sharp, sudden rise in blood alcohol may bring on a blackout when it reaches the brain. Slower consumption may ultimately bring on a higher blood alcohol level, but the elapsed time may allow the body to absorb and break down enough of the alcohol to prevent a surge from reaching the brain and causing the blackout.

If this theory is correct, food consumption helps prevent blackouts by slowing alcohol absorption.

Rule No. 2: *If a person wants to have a blackout, then by all means he should swill alcohol, the stronger the better, on an empty stomach as fast as he can. If he wants to avoid a blackout, then slow down the consumption, dilute the drinks, space them out, and above all eat.*

Words written centuries ago will introduce another factor in blackouts:

> *Methought I heard a voice cry, "Sleep no more!*
> *Macbeth does murder sleep,"–the innocent sleep;*
> *Sleep that knits up the ravell'd sleeve of care,*
> *The death of each day's life, sore labour's bath,*
> *Balm of hurt minds, great nature's second course.*
> *Chief nourisher in life's feast.*
>
> –Macbeth Act II

Shakespeare got it right. A good night's sleep is certainly all that. In ways not entirely understood, sleep somehow rests or retores the brain. Human beings need several hours of sleep each day. It varies with the person–Thomas Edison reportedly needed only two or three hours a day–but most people prefer seven or eight hours a day. However long a person sleeps, it must include the REM (Rapid Eye Movement) portions in which the brain dreams. Why sleep is important to brain function is not fully understood.

Sleep deprivation affects the whole brain. Every function deteriorates, motor skills, thought processes and judgment. If the person loses enough sleep she resembles at least a mildly inebriated person in walking, talking and thinking. If she is kept awake long enough, the cognitive brain functions will shut down entirely and she will be unable to stay awake, as in drunkenness.

Alcohol seriously disturbs sleep. The inebriated person quickly falls asleep, almost as soon as his head hits the pillow. Alcohol is a first cousin to ether, after all. Chances are he will sleep heavily for three or four hours, then fitfully thereafter. If he has REM sleep at all, it may not fit the normal pattern.

Rule No. 3: *If a person wants to increase his chances of a blackout, then by all means he should drink heavily when he is sleep deprived. If he wants to avoid a blackout, he should reduce his consumption when he is lacking sufficient sleep.*

A person on a "bender" risks a blackout. He has been drinking heavily for a couple of days or more. His amount of sleep is greatly reduced. Add alcohol in sufficient quantities–it may not actually take too much–and he becomes senseless in a blackout.

College students are at particular risk for blackouts. Many are sleep deprived, even chronically so. Then they engage in "binge drinking," atop of it. This may be considered a "recipe" for blackouts. Exam week is especially perilous. Students stay up to the wee hours all week, cramming for finals. After the exams, the keg is ordered. It is time to relax, celebrate, hang one on–and blackouts are likely to occur.

If a person has a history of blackouts, frequent periods when he cannot remember what went on, then it is imperative that he follow another rule:

Rule No. 4: *If he wishes to get into fights, commit crimes, or have accidents he knows nothing about, then he should be sure to go off alone while drinking. If he wishes to enjoy drinking and stay away from trouble, then he should not drink alone.*

To repeat for emphasis, the person in a blackout is not forming memory. He cannot remember anything for more than a moment or two. He cannot learn anything. If he makes a "decision," he cannot remember it long enough to act upon it, making his actions impulsive. His judgment is so impaired as to be nonexistent. Like Henry M., he cannot take care of himself and needs to be watched constantly. He is a menace to himself and others.

He should never be alone.

In case after case aloneness contributes to bizarre behavior. A 52-year-old man had successfully completed an alcoholic rehabilitation program in a West Coast city. He had been dry for 200 days and wanted to go home to introduce his family to the new man he had become.

He boarded a train for Portland, then apparently went to the club car to buy the new man a drink. The next thing he knows it's two days later and he's in jail with a broken tooth, black eye and multiple bruises. But he was sober enough to get back on the train. This time he made it all the way to Eugene, Oregon, before he blacked out. Finally he phoned friends who returned him to the recovery program where he'd started.

A housewife was unloading groceries from her van in front of her house. A man approached her, said he had a gun, then stole her van. Police were called and a search begun for the vehicle, which was found several hours later in front of a home. Inside, officers found an individual drunk and passed out. Investigation proved he not only had never had a gun, he had no memory of taking the van and driving it around for several hours. The guy was lucky. Since it was a first offense, he got off without jail time.

Kevin Price left the beach house alone, perhaps to retrieve his sleeping bag. If only someone at the party had said, "Hey, Kevin, where're you going?" and offered to join him for a breath of air, the tragedy might have been prevented. Even if the friend were drunk (but not blacked out) he might have remembered the sleeping bag as the reason for going outside. Even if this friend in his drunkenness agreed to go for a drive, he might well have asked where they were going and prevented the horrible wrong way turn-around on the parkway.

I have an idea that had Kevin's girlfriend been able to accompany him to the party instead of joining him the next day, the tragedy might have been averted.

Paul Cox left the accident alone. If his friends had decided to go with him or persuaded him to accompany them back to the bar for another drink, Paul Cox might have a different life today.

The blacked out person is probably at his most vulnerable when he goes off alone. His lack of short-term memory leaves him wholly susceptible to impulsive and irrational actions.

I suspect the incidence of accidents, injury and crime during blackouts would be higher, except that most drinking occurs communally. Drinking companions keep the blacked out person from harm, just by their presence, until he passes out or gets home safely.

There remains a problem associated with drinking and blackouts which companionship only aggravates. Michael Newbury illustrates it. Twenty-five at the time, living in Portland, Maine, he awoke on an April morning in 1992 to find blood everywhere, his girlfriend Rita Colucci beside him, her face beaten to an unrecognizable pulp from hammer blows.

Drunk and drenched in blood, Newbury tried to calm his nerves with more booze, then contemplated suicide. He phoned a friend to say, "I need a gun. I found Rita dead beside me and I don't remember anything." The friend convinced Newbury to summon the police instead. Veteran officers were sickened by the carnage in the apartment.

Eight months later Newbury pleaded guilty to manslaughter, continuing to say, "I was in an alcohol blackout. I don't remember anything."

The murder of Rita Colucci was hardly Newbury's first experience with not remembering. Blackouts were apparently common and frequent to him.

In September 1986, when he was 17, Newbury drove drunk, lost control of his car, hit a tree and killed his companion, Harold Huff. Newbury was sentenced to three years in prison.

During the three years he dated Rita Colucci, Newbury was arrested five times for assaulting her. Most of the time he was drunk when he attacked her.

The eventual murder of Rita Colucci, at least serious assault on her, was as predictable as the sunrise.

Harold Huff, Rita Colucci and especially Michael Newbury illustrate another rule of blackouts:

Rule No. 5: *If a person has a history of both blackouts and violence, he is a walking time bomb, a menace to those around him. If he wishes to avoid serious trouble, he should commit himself for treatment and never drink a drop of alcohol again. If this person, prone to both violence and blackouts, cannot keep himself from drinking, then society should find some way to do it for him.*

Rita Colucci, Harold Huff and even Michael Newbury himself are victims of law enforcement and judicial systems that did not understand the nature of blackouts, and how lethal they can be when they occur to a person with a history of both violence and blackouts.

It is one thing, like Kevin Price, to never have known about blackouts, and then have a horrific accident during his first one. It is quite another, like Michael Newbury, to have had a history of violence and blackouts, then drink to excess.

The murder of Rita Colucci suggests another rule of blackouts:

Rule No. 6: *If a person is female and for some bizarre reason likes being beaten up and raped, then she should drink till she blacks out. If a woman wishes to protect herself from such harm, particularly if she has had memory disturbances while drinking, then she had better either count her drinks or imbibe only with people she can trust.*

In the classic movie *The Thin Man,* there is a famous scene in which Nora Charles (played by Myrna Loy) arrives at the bar where her husband Nick (William Powell) has been drinking. She asks him how many drinks he's had, then she plays catch up, ordering the waiter to line up six dry martinis before her. The scene resonates a half century later as a blow for women's lib. What a man can do, a woman can do better.

I am in sympathy with and indeed support equal rights for women, but the ungarnished fact is that in general women do not handle alcohol as well as men. It has to do with physical size, liver weight and liver function. For her to belt down liquor as her men friends do is both foolish and dangerous.

Rita Colucci had a serious drinking problem. She tried to correct it and succeeded for some weeks. Then, on that April evening, she and Michael Newbury began to drink in their apartment.

Neighbors heard them quarreling, but then they often did that.

Rita Colucci was heard to scream, "Please, please, I love you, Mike." The sound of flesh striking flesh followed.

There may be a way for the Rita Coluccis of this world to recognize when the man they're with is in a blackout, unconscious and doesn't know what he's doing. They can at least try to escape him, especially if they know he has a tendency to violence. This is the subject of the next chapter.

8
Recognizing The Blackout

Our drinking friend from the last chapter has blacked out. She imbibed too much too fast on an empty stomach when she was sleep deprived. She doesn't know it and neither does anyone else. A couple of things must happen now to turn her into the walking, talking, unconscious subject of this book.

The blacked out person must greatly curtail consumption of alcohol. If she keeps on belting down the booze, she's going to lose her motor skills, stagger around, be obviously drunk to everyone around her, and soon pass out.

There are many reasons for an inebriated person to quit drinking. The bar closed. The host ran out of liquor, and all the package stores were shuttered. Or, her spouse or boyfriend warned her not to get drunk or insisted it was time to go home.

Like Kevin Price, perhaps, she felt nauseous and didn't want to drink any more. She became distracted, maybe by going to the powder room or talking to someone, and forgot where her glass was or even that she was drinking. Like Henry M., she has to be told to take a drink.

One of the time-honored ways to reduce consumption is to physically remove oneself from the liquor supply. Walk away from the bar or bottle. Abandon the glass and go across the room or out on the terrace and talk to other people. It happens a jillion times each day. It's a surefire way to slow down consumption.

There are lots of reasons to stop imbibing, including just not wanting any more to drink. Let's say our blacked out friend from the last chapter has a blood alcohol level (BAL) of 2.0. She's now at least quite mellow and thereby has little or no reason to drink further. *Drinking without thirst is a willful act, and willfulness implies volition, choice. Certain it is, the ability to choose is the last thing our blacked out friend has.*

The trigger for her to drink again is several hours away, after the liver has metabolized some of the alcohol in her system and alcoholic withdrawal starts. A friend may encourage her to have another drink, even pour one for her, but unless reminded, she will not remember it long enough to consume it.

One of the dangerous steps I'm taking in this unexplored terrain is to suggest that the act of blacking out tends to prolong the blackout by curtailing consumption, thus conserving procedural skills and enabling the blacked out person to continue to function, however marginally.

If studies of people in blackouts are ever begun again, I would like to just sit and watch them. How do they move, how do they act, what do they say? How much different are they from non-blacked out persons? Is there anything in their behavior that gives away their condition?

Because we do not know when a person has blacked out, and because that individual can never tell us what happened to him, we are left with anecdotal evidence. One much-published writer tells of waking the morning after a party. His host laughed at him and said, "I introduced you to people as a writer and one said, 'I sure hope he writes better than he talks.'"

Simply observing people is the stock in trade of psychology. My son, Daniel S. Sweeney, Ph.D., is a clinical psychologist specializing in play therapy. It's amazing to me what he does. He puts a child in a room filled with a variety of toys and other gear, then simply watches what the child plays with and how. From later talks with the child, he gains insights into what may be troubling the youngster. Would this methodology open some doors into the world of the blackout?

We sorely need psychologists to study blacked out persons to see what they say and do as a measure of brain functions. Studying the exact role of short-term or working memory in consciousness is of vital importance.

But which person is blacked out? We need some way to recognize him or her. Without it, research remains on hold. Our knowledge of blackouts and how to prevent and deal with them simply cannot advance until we have some way to detect the person in a blackout.

And it is not just for research purposes. Medical doctors, nurses and other hospital workers, especially in emergency rooms, and paramedics often depend on information provided by the patient in treating him. Where has he been, what's happened to him, what has he eaten or drunk? Such information can be vital for the patient's recovery. But the blacked out person may be able to give none of this or do so inaccurately. Medical personnel need training to spot the patient in a blackout and treat him accordingly.

Obviously it is vital for mental health workers, particularly in alcohol treatment centers, to recognize patients who have blacked out. Such recognition is also important to public health nurses, social workers and others in family counseling.

Bartenders and other purveyors of alcoholic beverages risk severe penalties when they sell to an inebriated person who then has an accident or commits a crime. They need some way to detect the blacked out person from the obviously drunken one.

Add law enforcement to the list. When the police stop a motorist suspected of driving under the influence, they administer a sobriety test. The driver may be asked to walk a straight line or to extend his arms, then touch his nose. In asking for his name and address the police listen for lisps, slurs and other manifestations of drunken speech. All of these are tests of coordination, motor skills as neurologists call them.

There is no doubt that intoxication deteriorates coordination. Since loss of motor control is more easily observed than loss of memory, cognition and judgment, we use staggering and slurring as the standard for drunkenness or sobriety, as that may be. Tests of it are written into the law.

Trouble is alcohol affects everyone differently. There are men and women who simply "hold their liquor" better than others. They do not stagger and slur. Indeed, they give no clear outward signs of drunkenness. Yet, they may be quite far gone, blacked out, perhaps close to passing out.

I am taking another step into the unknown, but I suspect it is possible for at least some blacked out people to pass a police sobriety test.

Again and again we have heard that persons in a blackout do not act as inebriated as the drunken ones. They move and talk, travel and drive apparently without incident. Again, the act of blacking out appears to reduce consumption of alcohol.

Society needs–I'm tempted to add the word *desperately*–some easily applicable test to detect the person in a blackout.

But those most in need of a way to detect blacked out people are the families and friends who must associate with them. Kevin Price's friends wish mightily they had realized his condition and taken his car keys from him. Rita Colucci–and how many others? –desperately wish they had known that their companion, the man they loved, was impulsive, irrational, and devoid of judgment. Michael Newbury might have been aware of hitting Rita Colucci at the moment he did it, but he apparently had no capacity to stop doing it or to remember doing it. He was beyond control.

Women need protection from blacked out partners. Society needs protection from blacked out drivers–and men prone to mindless violence.

Blacked out men and women need to be viewed as temporarily incapacitated, unable to look after themselves. They need the help and protection of friends and loved ones. The person in a blackout is a greater menace to himself and others than the obviously drunk person or certainly the passed out one.

Most spouses can tell when their husbands are drunk. One woman said she could see it in her husband's eyes, a sort of lack of focus or vacancy. Another woman said the "only way I can tell he's drunk is when he starts hitting me." But neither of these women could tell when he was blacked out. Most people can't detect it–especially the blacked out person himself.

We need a test for blackouts.

9
Three Little Words

As long as blackouts are simply considered a type of forgetfulness, Freudian repression or deliberate malingering, any sort of test is impossible. But with the new information that a blackout is interference with memory formation, tests to detect blackouts become possible, indeed rather easy.

We meet a couple at a cocktail party. Let's call them John and Marsha. Readers of a certain age may remember a novelty song by Stan Freberg called "John and Marsha." That was the entire lyric. A man and woman simply repeated the names over and over, along with gasps, sighs, giggles and other sounds, to convey various emotions, especially passion. It was cleverly done and amusing.

Let's assume it is some years later and John and Marsha are married. Marsha remains basically a normal drinker, nursing a highball or two the whole evening. John, on the other hand, has developed a drinking problem, tending to belt down booze mindlessly. That's a major reason Marsha doesn't drink. She has to look after him. Along with loving, honoring and obeying, she's the designated driver of this marriage.

The two are at a party doing their usual thing. Marsha is concerned about John. She has read this book and is worried that

John may have blacked out, something he's admitted doing before.

Marsha understands the way to detect a blackout is to test for short-term memory. Marsha now asks John about something that happened a short time ago. To avoid a quarrel, she does it casually and nonconfrontationally. "Who was that blonde (or guy) you were talking to a minute ago?" Or, "What were you and that fellow talking about? You sure were interested." Or, "Do you recall the name of that woman over there, we met her awhile ago, remember?" Or, "You're having a big laugh. What was so funny?"

If John has blacked out, he cannot remember something that happened a minute or two ago. His answers to the above questions may be, "What blonde? I wasn't talking to any blonde." Or, "I don't know what we talked about, nothing important." Or, "I never met the woman." Or, "A joke? Did somebody tell a joke?"

An even simpler way is for Marsha to interrupt or distract John while he is speaking, then come back to it. Everyone loses track of what they were saying occasionally, but if John does it consistently, then he may have blacked out.

At least Marsha may suspect her husband has a problem and begin to watch him more carefully.

But, clearly, a more refined test is needed, one bartenders, medical and social workers might administer to detect a blackout.

And the police.

Marsha should tell John that she has a test for him. Better yet, make a game of it. She might say, "John, dear, I don't think you're altogether here with the rest of us."

He denies it, of course. He's not drunk, he's fine.

Marsha says, "I'll bet if I told you something, you won't remember it five minutes later."

Being the sporting type, John accepts the challenge.

"I'm going to give you three words," Marsha says. Any three, preferably unrelated, will do. They don't have to be difficult. "Okay, John, the words are church, tiger and halfback. Can you remember them?"

"Of course, I can remember them."

"Then repeat them."

Using his immediate memory, he says, "Very well, church, tiger and halfback. What's so hard about that?"

"Just be sure you don't forget them."

"Okay, okay, I've got 'em, church, tiger, halfback."

Now Marsha distracts John. Perhaps she walks away from him for a while. A couple of minutes are enough, but make it five so the test is a good one.

Marsha returns and asks John about the little test he took. If he doesn't even remember taking the test, Marsha definitely has a blacked out husband. "The words I gave you, John, what were they?" If he comes up with all three or even two, he is not blacked out. Failure to repeat any word, or even just one, is a sure sign John has lost his short-term memory and is in a blackout.

I believe such a word test, even used on an informal basis, can permit detection of blackouts. Certainly bartenders can use it in determining when to cut off drinks. Anything will do, colors, trees, movies, movie stars, athletes, sports trivia, just so long as it is something newly learned, not known in the past.

If he can't remember something that happened a moment or two ago, then he has blacked out. The test may afford a way for a bartender, cop, physician or just a friend to appear to chat it up with an individual while determining whether he has blacked out.

But whoever gives the test, like Marsha, must be sober or close to it. Drunks aren't too reliable in testing other drunks.

Psychologists, educators and other experts should be able to devise a test of short-term memory that can be used in the field by police and other investigators.

The police have a legal method, the Breathalyzer Test, to determine when a person is drunk. It is accepted in court as proof of drunkenness. Surely, a legal way to determine a person has also blacked out can be developed.

I am expert neither in testing nor police procedures, but one way to test legally for a blackout might be for the police to carry a card on which several three or five word combinations are written. The officer asks the driver to be ready to repeat one of the combinations, then returns a couple minutes later to question him about the words. By encircling or underlining the words as the driver repeats them, the officer will have evidence usable in court to prove a blackout has occurred or not occurred. As we will see a little later, this can be an issue of profound importance.

Even without a formal test, police can suspect a blackout if they realize its nature. When police ask a suspected drunk driver for his name and address, our blacked out person will answer forthrightly. But if police ask him where he just came from or where he is going, now they may begin to discover a blackout.

So, Marsha has tested John and he has failed miserably, not even remembering the test, let alone any words. What does she do now?

Above all else Marsha should be aware of John's limitations. He may look and act only slightly inebriated, but he really doesn't know what he's saying or doing.

It is important for Marsha to stick to John like wet tissue. He simply cannot be allowed to wander off somewhere for some purpose only he knows and will forget in a moment. She doesn't want another Kevin Price. Get his car keys!

Marsha should be his constant companion, even enduring his inane conversations. Hopefully, she may be able to blunt some of his tactless remarks so as to prevent quarrels. In short, Marsha's task is to keep him out of the trouble he won't remember a second later.

In the process she must keep herself from taking offense at anything John says or does. The man is out of it. For Marsha to become angry and start a quarrel with John is to risk an escalation that she may well be unable to handle, particularly if the two of them have a history of marital discord.

When John is in a blackout is the worst possible time for Marsha to nag him about his drinking. It may lead to quarrels. And it's wasted effort, because he won't remember it the next day. When he's hung over, already swearing not to do it again might be the better time to discuss his drinking problem.

Marsha should try to get him home, or, if already home, try to get him to lie down and sleep awhile. But if this turns John belligerent, then she is probably wise to resign herself to partying on. Please, Marsha, don't give up on him and go home alone.

It may not be easy or a great deal of fun for her, but Marsha should treat John much as she would an unruly child. Like that child, he is not in control of and responsible for his actions. She needs to humor him, coax him and above all distract him. And hope for better days.

But, suppose John has a violent streak. In the past he has shoved Marsha around, threatened her, hit her. This night, Marsha has tried everything to distract him, laughing at his jokes, soothing his injured feelings. All has failed. He's picking a fight with her and she's unable to stop it.

What can Marsha do now?

She doesn't want to be alone with him, and she doesn't want him around the children. Since John is her husband and she loves him, Marsha doesn't want him driving a car or going off to bars alone. And she doesn't want to call the cops on him.

If she can't talk or distract him from his belligerency, and their mutual friends can't either, there remains one course of action, however regrettable it may be. Marsha should find his glass, put it in his hand, fill it up, the stronger the better, get him back to drinking, insist he have another, and keep it up till he can no longer stay awake and passes out. Remember he is a temporary Henry M. If you tell him it is time to drink, chances are he will.

As a physician I am loathe to tell anyone to deliberately get another person drunk until they pass out, but with a violent, blacked out man, it seems preferable over the alternative. How much better if Rita Colucci had known to get Michael Newbury passed out so he couldn't kill her. At the very least, trying to distract him with the joys of another drink, might give Rita Colucci and others in her position a chance to escape.

Bartenders in particular should realize that in dealing with the blacked out person, talk is so cheap it is worthless. Getting him to agree to go home to bed or some other course of action may be easily done, but he isn't going to remember it long enough to act on it. Allowing him get in his car and drive home is the worst thing to do. If a companion can't drive him home, then hopefully some cab driver will. Many cities have organizations of volunteers to drive the inebriated home from bars. If all else fails, calling the cops and letting him sleep it off in jail may be all that's possible.

I am a physician, specialist in internal medicine. In devising tests and counseling on the handling of drunks, I am invading fields of expertise far removed from my own. It is certainly lonely out here in unexplored territory. I wish I were not on this hike, but on a safari with lots of people helping me.

But blackouts do occur. At least some of the time the results are devastating. Pretending they do not occur or are simply benign phenomena, explainable under Freudian theory, simply adds to the problem. Whether it is a word test or some other measurement, we must find ways to recognize the blackout while it is occurring. Not until we do, can we study these people and keep them from harming themselves and others.

10
Are They Conscious?

Two couples were playing a rubber of bridge. Both men had been imbibing, just how heavily became apparent when one of them told a joke. This reminded the other man of a story, which he also told.

A few hands later, the first man remembered a joke he knew and told precisely the same story. This reminded the other man of a joke he knew, and he also repeated his same story–both within minutes.

Whatever else may be said about this bridge game, certain it is the wives had no need for a word test to determine blackouts. Repeating the same story (or information or opinion) is a sure sign short-term memory is gone and the person (in this case two people) has blacked out. They were like Henry M., riding in the car and repeating the same story every time he saw the MacDonald cup on the dashboard.

These two bridge players are sitting upright, talking, dealing, bidding and playing a difficult card game. To even suggest they are unconscious seems absurd. But is it absurd? This is the inquiry of this chapter.

The first question to be asked is whether the two men could play bridge while blacked out? Experienced players surely could, albeit not very well. Rules of the game, bidding practices, methods of play would all be stored in long-term memory, perhaps even in procedural memory, unaffected by a blackout.

But this pair should not be entered in international competition. Lacking short-term memory they would not remember their partner's bid for more than a few seconds. They would have to ask frequently for a review of the bidding–either that or make highly inappropriate bids. Our blacked out men would not be able to remember and count cards so as to really plan and play a hand. They would be "dummies," in more than one meaning of the word. Hopefully their partners would play most of the hands.

But are they unconscious? What is unconsciousness? And when is a person unconscious?

Unconscious may be applied to persons in a coma, or who have been knocked out by a blow to the head, or to those who have fainted or passed out from illness, alcohol or drugs. Simple sleep may be considered unconsciousness in the sense the sleeper lacks thoughts and feelings, even though he or she may be easily returned to consciousness. As in sleepwalking, the aroused person has no memory of what occurred while he slept.

Then there are various hypnotic and trancelike states where thought and feeling seem reduced. Persons in such states perhaps behave bizarrely or without their usual controls. Psychiatrists and psychologists also speak of fugue states or states of dissociation. The person is unaware or unable to control what he or she is doing.

Perhaps at the bottom of this continuum of consciousness is inattentiveness. A person is concentrating so hard on what she is reading, doing or thinking that she does not realize someone has entered the room and spoken to her. Here we have the celebrated absentminded professor, the spouse who doesn't listen and the child who doesn't hear you. We speak of them as "unconscious" of what is going on around them.

But what of our two bridge players and all other blacked out persons? Are they unconscious? It is an important question. We need to pursue an answer.

Every one of us is the sum total of our memories, everything that has ever happened to us and all that we have learned. Some people suggest that we even learn in the womb. There are those who claim to remember past lives. Still others believe we carry within our brain a cultural history of long ago events, even primeval knowledge obtained in the earliest days of the species. We may not consciously remember residing in trees, but we do recognize our fear of falling.

The very act of being conscious means to constantly summon up memory. Said another way, consciousness may be said to be a flow of memory, senses and thought. Writers speak of consciousness as a stream, ever flowing, constantly replenished. The only times it stops flowing is when we are anesthetized. Even in sleep it flows as an underground stream called dreams.

Writers, notably James Joyce and William Faulkner, have tried to put into words the mental ramblings of a stream of consciousness. I always found such writing difficult to read, simply because mental ramblings are by nature disorganized and meaningless. I look out my window and see a flowering shrub. Successive thoughts might be: the grass needs mowing, my mother's rose garden, cutting sticks for a wiener roast as a child, my wife's favorite color, pricking my finger on a thorn, it's time to give blood again.

There is an exercise said to improve memory. Try to recall, in order, the last five or ten or twenty thoughts that came into your head. It is not at all easy. Hopefully, it improves memory.

We all have this stream of consciousness. It is pure hypothesis on my part, undoubtedly unprovable, but I wonder if the thoughts, senses and memories called our stream of consciousness aren't vital to conserve brain function? Could this stream be a process for maintaining that intricate system of neurons, ganglia and synapses we call the human brain? The stream keeps the brain on "idle," ready for "action" the moment it is needed. Could that flowing stream be what keeps us conscious?

If we artificially interfere with the process, consuming sleeping pills, alcohol or drugs, we feel groggy or hung over the next day. After surgery, we go from the operating room to the "recovery" room, where we "come out" of anesthesia and our brain begins to function. Our first thought is "where am I?" We remember going to the hospital, being in the OR. We must be in recovery. We're okay. We're alive.

Memory allowed us to locate ourselves. Try to imagine what it might be like to wake up after surgery having no memory. We look at the walls, the light fixtures, window, bed, IV bottles, bandages, anything to try to figure out where we are, what we are doing and what has happened to us.

And while imagining that, try to conceive of the terror of Henry M. immediately following the surgery that removed his ability to form memory.

Finally, try to imagine Kevin Price waking up, trying to recognize where he was and how he got there. After all, the last thing he remembers was attending a party on the New Jersey shore. Fortunately his uncle was present to fill in some of the unremembered details, such as Kevin's traffic accident that killed five people. Worse, try to imagine the horror of Paul Cox when he learned two people were slashed to death in the house where he formerly lived during the time he was blacked out. Could he have done it?

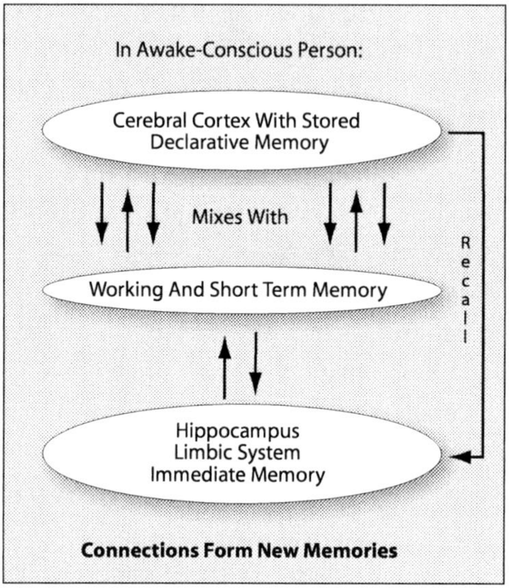

Fig. 4 Simplified Diagram of Working Memory

What Henry M. lost on a permanent basis and our card players, Kevin Price, Paul Cox and all others in blackout lose temporarily is what neuroscientists and psychologists now call *working memory.* (See Fig. 4)

When a person looks up a number in the phone book and holds it in his mind long enough to correctly dial it, he is using working memory. If this same person multiplies 12 times 52 in his head, he is using working memory. The very act of reading this sentence, certainly this paragraph, page, chapter and book involves working memory.

In his book *Synaptic Self,* Joseph LeDoux offers several illustrations of working memory. It allows a person to read a menu, keeping various options in mind, while listening to the specials announced by the waiter, then make up his mind, order and finally return to what was being discussed when the waiter appeared.

Working memory is surely needed to play board games like chess or Scrabble, as LeDoux suggests. It enables a person to look at a map and on that basis arrive at an unfamiliar location.

Working memory integrates immediate, short-term and long-term memory, allowing a person to create thought, reach a decision and take action. Working memory permits an individual to hold on to a sense impression or a bit of information while related memories and information are recalled from long-term memory.

To understand working memory, let's suppose Ed and Bill, good friends and neighbors, are chatting over the back fence. Bill says, "My boss gave me two tickets to Sunday's game. Wanna go, Ed?"

Simple question, but before Ed can answer a host of information must be retrieved from his memory–almost instantly. Let's consider a few.

What game? Could be poker. But they play that on Friday nights. Could be a Little League game both their sons play in. But Ed said tickets. No tickets needed for little league. Could be pro football or pro basketball. Both play on Sunday. But Ed's working memory provides a quick answer to which game. It's summer. Neither football nor basketball is being played. Bill wears a blue cap with a certain letter on it. And Ed knows Bill is a rabid fan of that team. Bill has tickets to a Los Angeles Dodger game.

At once Ed's brain recalls images of baseball being played, Dodger Stadium and pleasant memories of other games attended there, his father who took him, his own son who went once. He thinks of what plans he has for Sunday; how his wife and son will feel if he goes off to a game without them; what parking, hotdogs, beer etc. will cost and can he afford it and ought he to spend the money; the weather forecast for Sunday; the state of the pennant races and who the Dodgers are playing.

Ed looks at his friend. It's two in the afternoon and Bill has already had a few. The last time they went to a game together, Bill got pretty loud and boisterous. Wasn't much fun.

Infinitely more senses, memories and thoughts race through Ed's mind. Thus are present and past integrated in working memory. Should he go? He hesitates a fraction of a second, then replies,

"I better take a rain check, Bill. I promised Ellen and Sean we'd do something together." He hadn't but he will now–a fact now stored in his memory.

For a student, the very process of learning is an exercise in working memory. She must hold in her memory a piece of information while determination is made whether she already knows that or is it new information. Then it must be cataloged for later retrieval. The pieces of information continue to be held, perhaps sentence-by-sentence, as she reads and learns. Then all the information is recalled, regurgitated, and organized so she can write a paper for her teacher or professor.

During exam week students routinely cram quite remarkable amounts of information into their working memory, quite often recalling a good bit of it years later.

The existence of working memory, in substantial degree, is what makes us Homo Sapiens.

The concept of working memory originated with psychologist Alan D. Baddeley. He described working memory as allowing humans to comprehend and mentally represent their immediate environment, to retain information about their immediate past experience, to support the acquisition of new knowledge, to solve problems, and to formulate, relate and act on current goals.

Since Baddeley offered his hypothesis in the mid-1980s, study of working memory has greatly expanded. The Google search engine of the Internet lists millions of papers on working memory. In large part, these studies seek to locate specialized areas of the brain where memory is stored or where working memory activities (language, calculation, emotion) occur. The concept of working memory has grown to include the activities of an "executive" in the cortex to direct the activities of working memory.

These studies are valuable, but for our purpose of understanding the effects of alcohol blackouts on working memory we need to simplify, not complicate the process. For example, many psychologists now use the term working memory instead of short-term memory. Immediate memory is also included in working memory. Indeed, that is correct. Immediate memory and short-term memory feed into working memory.

But if we are to understand the devastating effects of alcohol on working memory, we must differentiate between immediate and short-term memory.

Look at Fig. 4. Senses and new information become immediate memory. (The seat of immediate memory is unknown, perhaps the amygdala, located near the hippocampus in the mid-brain.) From immediate memory, the sense impression or piece of information goes to the hippocampus, where it is transferred to short-term memory using the NMDA neurotransmitters.

Short-term memory is believed stored in the temporal lobe, located in the mid-brain, just above the hippocampus. While the information is held there, a stream of other, older memories and information flow from stored or long-term memory in the cerebral cortex. The information in the temporal lobe and in the cerebral cortex flow back and forth, current impression or information influencing or being influenced by past memory, resulting in thought, decision and action.

This is working memory, and it occurs more or less constantly in a conscious person.

Perhaps the best description was given by Dr. Leslie Ungerleider, Chief of the Laboratory of Brain and Cognition of the National Institute of Mental Health: "Working Memory is an essential building block of our cognitive abilities, from mental arithmetic to logical reasoning." He adds: "*Working memory–what we're aware of from one moment to the next–bridges time and is the content of our consciousness.*" (Emphasis mine)

Now add alcohol. What happens to working memory, the

"content of our consciousness?" Very little at first. A drink or two may seem even to aid the process by relaxing us and lowering inhibitions. A person's memory seems sharper, his repartee brighter—at least to himself.

What happens if consumption continues? As described in Chapter Five, alcohol affects the entirety of the brain. All its functions begin to deteriorate. The drinker can speak, but it is now slurred. He can walk, but he is unsteady on his feet. He can remember, but he tends to fixate on one thought, often repeating it over and over. His working memory still functions, but often what is remembered is shallow, repetitious, inane, even stupid. Sober people recognize him as drunk and not himself.

Hopefully this fellow goes home to bed and sleeps it off. But suppose he blacks out. What happens to working memory now?

He becomes Henry M. for a time.

Alcohol does temporarily to our drinker what the surgeon did to Henry permanently. The link between immediate memory and short-term memory is severed. (See Fig. 5.) Sights, sounds, words, thoughts, information are known to both Henry and the blacked out person—but only fleetingly, a few seconds, at best a

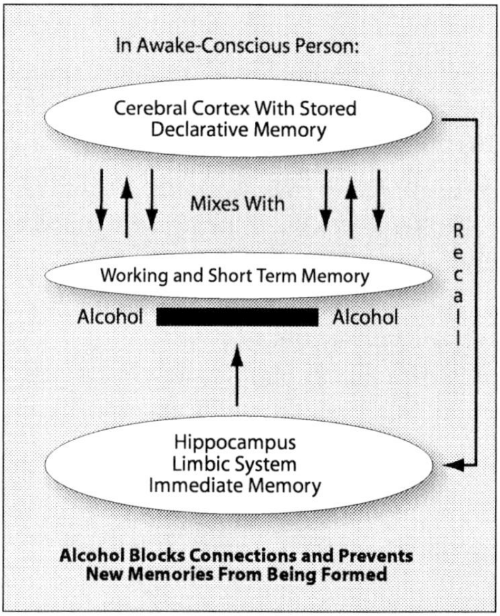

Fig. 5 Simplified Diagram of Working Memory Inhibited by Alcohol

minute or two, however long it can be retained in immediate memory.

Alcohol has shut down the NMDA receptors in the hippocampus. Nothing reaches short-term memory. Working memory, that "content of our consciousness," has been short-circuited. The stream of consciousness has been dammed up.

The person in a blackout cannot hold any fact, sense impression or thought in his head long enough to make use of it to solve a problem and decide on action. Asking him to multiply 12 times 52 in his head is to ask an impossibility.

He may be able to phone home or some other number he knows very well, but asking him to look up and remember a seven digit number long enough to dial it is a futile exercise.

He is not going to read and understand anything, learn anything, decide anything, act any other way than instinctively. He has no forethought, no sense of consequences and how to avoid them, no ability to plan, no awareness of how his impulses may relate to anything else. He is the proverbial loose cannon.

When he talks, the blacked out person more closely resembles a child than an adult. My grandson, Bryce Neimond, learned to speak before he could control his speaking. He would utter whatever he was thinking. It came out verbally as understandable words, even phrases, but in fact made no real sense. It was not a stream, but a torrent of his cognitive moments, switching from one thought to another without hesitancy and so rapidly he could not be followed. He was jabbering. This is understandable in a child, indeed useful as a learning process, but in an adult? We all know the answer.

What are the capabilities of a person in a blackout? His procedural memory is intact. Except to the degree drunkenness has impaired his motor skills, he can drive a car, ride a bicycle, walk, swim, have sex, talk in the sense of jabbering, etc. If he hasn't gone somewhere else while blacked out, he knows where he's at, where he lives and how to get home. But he doesn't have a prayer of whether he should drive himself there in his present condition. He doesn't even know what his condition is.

He can recall specific facts from long-term memory in his cortex, but they do not relate to anything he recently learned–and they remain only fleetingly. He recalls a joke from his long-term memory, then repeats it to the same person, because he can't remember he just told it. He remembers long held opinions and information, reciting them over and over, perhaps in a loud voice. He seldom listens, because to hear something and relate it to other information requires working memory. He has none.

If he meets someone new, he will not remember her more than a minute or two. If she gives him directions to her house, he will not remember the directions or that he was given them. If he writes the directions down, he will not remember where they are to take him and why. If his long-term memory informs him he is supposed to go to Chicago (or El Paso, Nassau or Timbuktu) he may well decide he'd better head for the airport. And suppose his job is airline pilot.

Our blacked out person, lacking working memory, is a wanderer through life, lost, living from moment to moment, unmotivated, unable to learn, unaware of his own diminished capacities, a clear and present danger to himself and others.

Is this blacked out person conscious? This is our bottom line.

I looked up both conscious and unconscious in medical dictionaries. Mosby defined unconscious as: "unaware of the surrounding environment; insensible; incapable of responding to sensory stimuli." Similarly conscious was defined as: "(in neurology) capable of responding to sensory stimuli; awake, alert; aware of one's external environment."

The Stedman dictionary said consciousness is "a state of awareness, implying that the individual is oriented to time and place, and person (i.e., knows approximate the date, the nature of the environment, his or her name, and other pertinent personal data). Consciousness combines memories and the comprehension of external reality, as well as the person's emotional status and goals."

Under the definition in the Mosby dictionary, the blacked out person is probably conscious. He is awake, alert, aware of his external environment, "capable of responding to sensory stimuli."

Under the definition in the Stedman's dictionary the person in a blackout is conscious in that he is "oriented to time and place." He knows his name, other personal data.

But then Stedmen's goes on to say, "Consciousness combines memories and the comprehension of external reality, as well as the person's emotional status and goals." That certainly does not make our blacked out person conscious. He has little awareness of external reality and no goals other than impulses.

In his book *Essential Sources in the Scientific Study of Consciousness*, Dr. Bernard J. Baars says that for consciousness to occur, three things must happen. The reticular activating system of the brain must be operating. In easier words, the person must be awake. Then, the thalamus must be operating to open and close (control) sensory tracts. Finally, *stimuli must be remembered.* (emphasis mine) Dr. Baars seems to see memory as integral to consciousness.

In his book *Wider than the Sky*, Gerald M. Edelman M.D. writes that "consciousness requires us to be conscious of being conscious." He distinguishes between "primary consciousness" (a state of being aware of our surroundings) and "higher order consciousness" (remembering past episodes and creating future intentions.) The latter requires primary consciousness, but awareness does not require higher order consciousness.

Many other sources could be cited. All reveal an ongoing struggle to understand and define consciousness. Yet all of them include wakefulness, awareness and memory.

I have compared the blacked out person to Henry M. Therefore, the question must be asked: Is Henry conscious? He fails Baars' test. He is awake, but he cannot remember stimuli.

Henry is awake, functioning, living a life. But it is a carefully proscribed life. He lives in a nursing home, where he is protected and looked after. He has little sense of time and place. He cannot order his affairs, remember a schedule, decide when to eat or go to bed. Society recognizes that he cannot live by himself. His ability to remember and learn is so curtailed (and not of his own doing) that others must take care of him.

The same identical words may be applied to the person in a blackout–except that it was of his own doing. He bent his elbow. He consumed the alcohol. But knowing the cause and assessing blame does not alter the central fact: *This person cannot take care of himself and must be looked after.*

One more time, is the person in a blackout unconscious?

If we look elsewhere for a definition, perhaps lexography can lead us to an answer. In various dictionaries, a person is said to be conscious if:

- He perceives, apprehends or notices with a degree of controlled thought or observation;
- He is capable of thought, will, design or perception;
- He has mental faculties undulled by sleep, faintness or stupor;
- He acts with critical awareness;
- He is aware of his own existence, sensations, thoughts and surroundings;
- He has mental faculties fully active;

- He is aware of what he is doing;
- His actions are intentional and deliberate.

Our blacked out person fails on all these counts. He is not conscious. He is blacked out. He must be dealt with as we would anyone of diminished capacity.

A goodly amount of the research being performed on working memory—those two million-plus publications listed on the Google search engine—relates to the hunt for human consciousness. Where in our brain does our self-awareness lie? What in our heads makes us constantly aware of where we are, what we are doing? How is it possible for us to study the very organ that enables us to study that organ? These questions are major puzzles in science.

I wonder if carefully controlled studies of the alcohol blackout might not expand our knowledge of consciousness. If EEGs, PET scans, MRIs and other modern techniques were applied to persons known to be in an alcohol blackout, it is just possible our knowledge of consciousness and brain function might be enhanced.

One thing is certain. None of it will ever happen as long as the alcohol blackout is considered forgetting, malingering or Freudian repression. The persistence of these anachronistic attitudes has far too long inhibited serious study of what is both a public health problem and an avenue for understanding brain function.

11
Dr. Jekyll Meet Mr. Hyde

In the 1886 tale by Robert Lewis Stevenson, Dr. Jekyll is well-mannered and dignified, respected as a physician and scientist, much loved by his fiancée and friends. Yet, Dr. Jekyll is conscious of the mixture of good and evil in his own nature.

Working secretly in his laboratory, Dr. Jekyll concocts a potion that creates a separate personality which absorbs all the evil in a person's nature. Dr. Jekyll secretly drinks the potion and turns into Mr. Hyde, a person of pure evil. Mr. Hyde runs off into the night and performs nefarious deeds, but a few hours later the potion wears off and he becomes kindly, wise Dr. Jekyll.

Eventually Jekyll loses control, returning involuntarily to Hyde. Evil triumphs over virtue. When Hyde commits a horrible murder and Jekyll faces discovery and arrest, he kills himself.

There is something about this gothic tale, which resonates within all of us. Do we have a dark side, lurking below the surface, which threatens in a moment of weakness to subsume our virtue? Many novels probe the question. Sigmund Freud was much taken with the concept, calling his dual forces Id and Ego. Various religions both identify sin and ways to combat it. Certain it is that enough good people fail to resist temptation often enough to keep the old Jekyll-Hyde story timely.

Is alcohol the potion that changes virtue into evil? More to the point of this book, is a person more apt to commit a crime in an alcohol blackout than he is while sober?

Unequivocally, the answer has to be yes. The blacked out person has the diminished inhibitions and motor control associated with drunkenness. In addition he has lost his working memory and with it his ability to learn, reason, plan and form goals. We have said repeatedly a blacked out person is a menace to himself and others.

But does the blacked out Dr. Jekyll become the evil Mr. Hyde, bent on mayhem and crime?

There is no shortage of cases in which alcohol brought out Mr. Hyde. We have already considered Michael Newbury who viciously hammered Rita Colucci to death while in an alcohol blackout.

Not too far away in Biddleford, Maine, 20-year-old Devon O'Brien went to a bar where he met a man named Steven Schoff, Jr., 26. After a time spent drinking, the two left in Schoff's car. They wound up at a gravel pit where Schoff shot O'Brien three times. Schoff would later explain in court that he drank so much that night, he couldn't remember much of anything.

What began as an argument in a St. Albans, W. Va., bar between Sonya and Christopher Bailey, ended six days later in a Corbin, Ky. hospital. Bailey beat his wife into unconsciousness that first night, locked her in the trunk of her car, then drove back and forth between the two states for six days, never seeking medical attention for his wife. Sonya Bailey lapsed into a coma and remains in a vegetative state.

Christopher Bailey contended he was in an alcohol blackout and never meant to hurt his wife. He testified that he was not sure if he had inflicted his wife's injuries. He could only remember coming out of the blackout and finding his wife's bloody body. He said he was afraid to seek medical care for his wife for fear of being questioned.

In 1981, Marjorie E. Deeble was found dead in her Los Alamitos, California, home. Her partially clothed body was secured to a dresser by a belt looped around her neck. She had been beaten, mutilated and raped.

Mrs. Deeble was the mother of a former girlfriend of Robert Mark Edwards. But police had no evidence linking him to the crime until 12 years later, in 1993, when a woman in Maui, Hawaii, was murdered under similar circumstances. Edwards lived near the woman. His bloody handprints and footprints were at the scene. Edwards was then convicted of the earlier murder of Mrs. Deeble. At that trial Edwards claimed, through his lawyer, that he was in an alcohol blackout during each murder and doesn't remember them. He was sentenced to life in prison.

James Edward Reid, 51, awoke one morning to find blood on his clothes. Nearby was the body of Annie V. Lester, brutally murdered. Police quickly found overwhelming circumstantial evidence linking Reid to the crime, including fingerprint and DNA matches and handwriting samples. Confronted by the evidence, Reid pleaded guilty.

At his sentencing Reid's attorney presented evidence that Reid had blacked out during the crime. Reid had suffered brain damage in a traffic accident that left him in a coma for five days. Thereafter, that part of Reid's brain that affects personality and impulse control was damaged. Also, Reid was an alcoholic and a binge drinker. Three medical experts testified to Reid's tendency to blackout when intoxicated and his inability to perform intentional acts during the blackouts. Family members and friends verified this. And it was testified Reid, when sober, was a calm, kind, and conscientious person.

Reid was sentenced to death.

Dick Fekete, 55, was a highly regarded agent with the federal Drug Enforcement Administration. In December 1997, Fekete awoke from a car accident, not knowing what had happened. Among his first words were "Who did I kill?"

In the crumpled wreckage of the government car police found the bullet-ridden body of Shaun Curl, 42, a fellow DEA agent. Curl had offered a drunken Fekete a ride home from an all-day Christmas party. Curl left behind a wife and two young children.

Fekete pleaded guilty to manslaughter and was sentenced to 15 years in prison. Fekete says he was in an alcohol blackout, one of several he experienced that were marked by violence. He says he doesn't know that he shot Curl. He has no recollection of doing it.

Two other cases need to be added to this list. Gary Gauger was accused in 1993 of murdering his parents at their Illinois farm. Paul Cox was accused of murdering a husband and wife, both doctors, in their beds. Cox had formerly lived in the murder house.

The Gauger and Cox cases will figure prominently in pages to come. Both men claimed they were in a blackout and had no knowledge of the murders for which they were charged and convicted.

This is a rather grisly list, suggesting that Mr. Hyde is alive and well among blacked out persons. Perhaps, but the list is most notable for its brevity. I spent many hours over several days perusing the Internet for murders in which a claim of blackout was clearly made. There are perhaps a few, more-questionable cases, but this is basically the entire list. Since my search covered several years, it must be assumed many thousands of murders were committed in the United States during that period. Yet, only a relative handful involved a claim of blackout.

This could be a result of poor research on my part. Or, it could be the failure of reporters to place importance on blackout claims and thus fail to report them in news stories. It is perhaps more likely that defense attorneys do not very often bring up blackout as a defense. It has no legal standing. In the U.S., when a person swallows the first drop of alcohol, he or she is legally responsible for whatever else happens.

One other possibility comes to mind. Maybe murder and mayhem isn't that common among blacked out folks. Perhaps Mr. Hyde doesn't show up among these people any more often than he does among those in possession of their faculties. We need to examine this.

Whatever else he is, the blacked out person is a lousy murderer. The image of the out-of-his-mind zombie stalking his platinum-haired prey is okay in horror movies, but it will never happen in real life. The person in a blackout can't stalk anyone. If he sets out to do it, he won't remember what he is supposed to be doing for longer than a few paces. He'll just be a guy going for an aimless walk.

Again, the person in a blackout is incapable of forming intent. Chances are this fellow doesn't have enough sense to come in out of the rain, let alone plan to kill someone. If he's standing outside in a downpour, he might find it unpleasant and seek relief. From his long-term memory he might recall going into a building when it rained. But neither of those bits of information would enter his working memory to lead to a decision to run for cover. Unless someone rescues him or he accidentally finds shelter, the blacked out wretch will stand out there being drenched.

The same may be said for a blacked out person walking on a railroad track. He may see and hear the train coming, and he may know to get off the track, but those pieces of information will never combine in working memory to form a plan. Without a plan he cannot form intent.

The person in a blackout is incapable of murder. By legal definition, murder involves intent. The blacked out person cannot formulate intent. Without it, the worst he can do is manslaughter. That's a nitpicky distinction to the victim and his or her loved ones, but it is of monumental importance to judges, juries and lawyers.

If the blacked out person kills someone, it just has to be an impulsive act. The perpetrator has been drinking–perhaps the victim has, too. Alcohol has lowered inhibitions. Civility is strained. Nasty words are uttered, tempers flare, violence erupts. He or she lashes out in a rage, swinging a fist, perhaps one containing a knife, gun or other weapon, and mindlessly kills a person. How many times a day is a scenario something like this played out?

Our blacked out Dr. Jekyll may not be able to plan a murder–or come in out of the rain–but he is quite capable of anger and rage. He is expert at cat-fights, shoving matches, fisticuffs, brawls and other forms of mayhem. If some kind of weapon gets into his hand, he can kill. No doubt about it.

To repeat, when a person suspects a spouse or companion is blacked out–or maybe just inebriated–this is not the time for criticism, button-pushing or quarrel-picking. This is the time for soothing words, expressions of affection, abundant yes-dears, followed by why-don't-we-go-to-bed-and-talk-about-it-tomorrows.

Again, is alcohol the potion that turns Dr. Jekyll into Mr. Hyde? It really has never been studied and it needs to be–desperately. We don't know why one man becomes violent while another, equally angry perhaps, turns his back and walks away.

Hitting a woman is a taboo of long standing among men. Just how long is a worthy question. It might date back to the days of chivalry and the knights of yore, when women were to be protected and rescued from dragons. But I suspect it goes much further back. Even the earliest man realized the importance of females to bear and raise children, the seed of his loins. The children need their mother for several years if the species is to survive. Protecting women and children is a biological imperative.

Fast forward to the 20th century. In the charming old movie *Father Goose,* Leslie Caron and some children are stranded on a Pacific isle with a grubby Cary Grant, a coast watcher during World War II. At one point Ms. Caron slaps Grant, then he instantly slaps her back. That's the first moment they know they are in love.

As they say, that's Hollywood. What happens in real life, had these two been real people, is that Ms. Caron may slap Mr. Grant all right. That's permissible. He becomes angry and raises his hand to her, hesitates, then slowly lowers the hand and walks away.

Something goes on in the head of a normal, mature, adult male which prevents him from physically harming a woman. If he does harm her, there is something wrong with him. The same statement may be made in even stronger fashion in regards to children–and is just as true of women as men. And it is equally true of lions, tigers, elephants, most mammals, and indeed the majority of all species.

So, the man–let's call him Mr. Hyde–who physically attacks a woman is an anomaly in his species. He really should seriously wonder what's wrong with himself and seek treatment. Hopefully some is available.

But the taboo doesn't just apply to women and children, does it? Society has a rigorous taboo against killing anyone. If we didn't, the streets would run with blood and bodies would be everywhere.

The crimes of murder, manslaughter, vehicular or involuntary manslaughter are severely punished. If the murder is heinous and he is sentenced to death, that is also controversial and protested as legalized murder. Among the industrialized nations, the United States alone administers the death penalty.

It is not just the fear of punishment that keeps us from murder. Killing anyone, even accidentally, is traumatic for most people, as many involved in traffic deaths can attest. Some never get over it.

How about war? Combat has certainly justified enough killing through the ages. But most soldiers in modern combat do not see their enemy. Bombs are dropped, artillery fired, machine guns and rifles shot. But the victims are seldom seen. The shooting, firing and dropping are impersonal acts, justified as self-defense and war.

But what happens when it becomes personal? A combat veteran tells this story. In 1952 he was at age 19 a platoon sergeant, a veteran of many engagements in the Korean War, the so-called "forgotten war." His unit was now holding a strategic hilltop north of the 38th Parallel, when the Chinese Red Army attacked in force, nearly overwhelming the Americans and South Koreans.

Just as the order to fall back came, a Chinese soldier jumped into the sergeant's foxhole. Let him tell the story: "He was a kid, even younger than I was. It seemed an eternity that we looked at each other. In his eyes was the same fear I felt."

The sergeant held a .45 automatic in his hand, taken off a dead comrade.

"I was supposed to kill the enemy. It was my job, what I was trained to do. I shot him between the eyes and got the hell out of there."

This sergeant returned home, went to college, launched a successful career in business, married and raised a family. But he never forgot that face or those eyes. Years later, he succumbed to alcoholism, became alienated from his family. The Veterans Administration diagnosed him as having post-traumatic stress syndrome from his war experiences and pensioned him as a disabled veteran.

One other fact about this man is notable. In all the years after that foxhole incident, he never again fired a weapon or lifted a hand to anyone. He remains a staunch advocate of nonviolence. He joined marches protesting the War in Vietnam and remains anti-war to this day. He's against the death penalty.

This man's experience is anything but unique. Millions of combat veterans have had similar feelings. Only in recent years has it come out that veterans of World War II, the so-called "good war," suffered from post-warfare aberrations of the most debilitating sort. The war's most decorated soldier, Audie Murphy, the actor, suffered agonizing nightmares throughout his life.

The point is that even men trained in combat with a justification to kill find it difficult and debilitating to do so. Just how difficult has been studied, with surprising results.

During World War II, S.L.A. Marshall, then an army officer, questioned about 400 U. S. Infantrymen in the Pacific and European theaters. He found that on average less than 15 per cent of the men had fired at enemy positions or personnel with rifles, grenades, machine guns or other weapons.

In World War II and the Korean War, soldiers tended to fight individually from personal foxholes. When others watched them, as in machine gun crews or mortar squads, they tended to fire their weapons.

Another study by Lt. Col. Dave Grossman produced even more startling information about the Battle of Gettysburg in the Civil War. At that time soldiers attacked or defended shoulder to shoulder. Everyone was watched. Did everyone fire? Not hardly. After the battle 27,574 muskets were recovered. Of these, Grossman reports, nearly 90 per cent (24,000) were loaded but not fired. Of these, 12,000 had more than one bullet in the barrel–and 6,000 had from three to ten rounds loaded in the barrel. One unfired weapon had been loaded 23 times!

This could occur because the muskets were muzzle loading. The process was to pour black powder down the barrel, drop in a bullet, ram the bullet home with a rod, prime, cock, raise the weapons to the shoulder and fire. Clearly, many soldiers at Gettysburg, marching shoulder to shoulder with their comrades, loaded their weapons but did not fire them–often over and over.

None of these men in any of the wars were cowards. All were in battle, risking their lives, in a position to be killed. So why didn't they shoot? Because it violates the moral code and ideals of civilized society. From birth he has been taught that taking of life is prohibited and unacceptable. Try as it will, the Army can change that only with the greatest difficulty.

Another story indicates just how difficult it is. After the Marshall and Grossman studies, the military changed its training techniques. Instead of using firing ranges, recruits were put to shooting at pop-up targets under simulated battle conditions. This apparently worked. The Army reported 90 per cent of the soldiers fired their weapons in the War in Vietnam.

Fired at what? Did they fire at the enemy or into the air? Long known to the military, it is called "posturing." Grossman studied the ratio of bullets fired to enemy dead. In earlier wars the ratio ranged from 13 to 1 to 252 to l. In Vietnam the ratio was more than 50,000 to one. Lots of firing, little result.

If trained and motivated men cannot or will not shoot at an

enemy, how difficult must it be for the average person to raise a hand, pick up some kind of weapon and kill another human being?

Something other than moral restraint is at work in the healthy, adult Dr. Jekyll. Students of the human brain call it emotional memory. To understand it, recall Henry M. and an incident in Chapter Four. A researcher carried a pin in his hand, which pricked Henry as they shook hands. The next day Henry had no idea who the fellow was as they met again, but Henry refused to shake his hand. That is emotional memory.

We do not hold our hand in the fire because of emotional memory of what it feels like to be burned. Nor do we place our thumb on a board and allow someone to swing a hammer at it–not if we can help it. We do not jaywalk across a super-highway at rush hour, stick our toe in boiling water, tell the dentist we do not need anesthetic while he's drilling. Et cetera, et cetera.

Nor do we pick a fistfight, because, among other reasons, we might get hit back and that can hurt. Even if we've never been to jail or prison, we know it as unpleasant. Hence we scrupulously obey the law to hopefully avoid the place. Being sick is no fun, so we try to avoid accidents, take care of ourselves and go to the doctor for checkups.

As far as is known, emotional memory functions in a blackout. Suppose Kevin Price didn't know how to drive and came to the party with a friend. He might then have gone out to the car to get the sleeping bag so he could go to sleep. But if he didn't know how to drive, emotional memory would have prevented him from getting behind the wheel, even if the keys were in the car.

Primal restraints, moral codes and emotional memory have hardly turned society into saints. From the Holocaust to today's headline, we know with certainty and fear that violence does occur, hideously and frequently. It might even be said to occur incessantly.

Why this happens is not something we need to consider deeply in this book. It may be caused by *operant conditioning.* He was beaten or saw a great deal of violence as a child. He may have a neurological dysfunction in his brain that induces him to violence. I'm sure there are many other causes of violence including various drugs.

And there is alcohol.

If it only makes a person mellow, another talkative and giddy, no harm in either case. But suppose this imbiber bears some resentment against his wife, neighbor, or boss. Inhibitions are lowered and the tongue loosened. He is at risk of saying things he may later wish he hadn't. There is some possible harm now.

If alcohol makes him hypersensitive, defensive, argumentative, quarrelsome, he and especially those around him need to be careful. Lots of harm can occur now in the form of marital discord, lost friendships, unemployment.

Suppose, God forbid, this drinker has a streak of violence in him. He has a history of shoving matches, bar fights, brawls, and other mindless and worsening violence. Such a person should not drink at all.

At the apex of this continuum are the persons like Michael Newbury, Steven Schoff, Jr., Christopher Bailey, Robert Mark Edwards, James Edward Reid, Dick Fekete and others with a history of both blackouts and violence. They are every one Mr. Hyde.

What can be concluded from all this? Again, we desperately need research. Without it only a hypothesis is possible. Mine is that alcohol and blackouts of themselves do not create violence, turning the amiable Dr. Jekyll into the evil Mr. Hyde. If it did, our streets would run with blood and alcohol would have to be banned.

But there are people with a proclivity toward and a history of violence who should not drink, indeed, be allowed to drink. If the state cannot keep them from it, then their family, friends and associates must be careful around them and avoid them if at all possible.

If you are a woman and the man you live with hits you, drunk or sober, then move out at once. If you are a man who hits a woman, drunk or sober, then seek treatment at once.

12

If Only The Jury Had Heard...

Let's return now to the Paul Cox case, first described in Chapter Two. To review, in November 1994, a jury in Westchester County, N. Y. convicted Cox of two counts of manslaughter in the deaths of Drs. Rao and Shanta Chervu on December 31, 1988. Cox was sentenced to a term of 33 to 100 years in prison.

More than any other I know, the Cox trial illustrates the societal difficulties associated with blackouts. No one involved in the case knew the true nature of a blackout, not Cox, his family, his attorney; not the police, the prosecutor, the judge; none of the witnesses, certainly not the jurors.

The question to be considered here is this: Did the ignorance of those involved in the trial bring about a miscarriage of justice?

Let me point out at the outset that I have a distant familial relationship to Cox. His mother Mary is the sister of my brother's wife. I met Paul on one occasion in the 1980s at a large family garden party at his parent's home. He would have been a teenager. I honestly don't remember him. I did not see him again until August 2003 in preparing this book.

I have no vested interest in the Cox case. I don't know whether he is guilty or not. He may have done these ghastly crimes. My entire reason for delving into the Cox case is to point out that without knowledge of the true nature of blackouts no correct verdict could be reached.

What was the case against Cox, as presented by the prosecution? After a night of heavy drinking, the 21-year-old Cox, ran his mother's car into a guardrail in Larchmont, N. Y. Walking home in the wee hours of December 31, 1988, he allegedly went to the home where he lived prior to age seven, broke a pane of glass and entered the kitchen.

He now supposedly selected a large butcher knife from a rack on the kitchen counter and went upstairs, where he found the Drs. Chervu asleep in bed. He stabbed Lakshman Rao Chervu 15 times, mostly about the upper body and heart, and slashed at Shanta Chervu nine times, eventually cutting her throat. On the way to his home, Cox supposedly got rid of the murder weapon so it was never found. Perhaps he threw it into the nearby Long Island Sound.

A major problem for Prosecutor George L. Bolen—and most especially two juries—was motive. Why would Cox brutally murder two people he didn't know? At one point Bolen suggested the drunken Cox entered the Chervu home bent on robbery, where Mrs. Chervu confronted him. Cox grabbed the knife and Mrs. Chervu ran upstairs to her husband. Cox followed and slew them both.

But mostly Prosecutor Bolen, strangely joined by Defense Counsel Andrew Rubin, maintained that Cox mistakenly slew the Chervus, believing he was stabbing to death Frank and Mary Cox—his father and mother.

Most of the testimony in both trials dealt with psychiatric issues. Both prosecution and defense portrayed Paul Cox as a young man who underachieved in a wealthy and successful family. His repeated failures in school supposedly led to parental disapproval and rejection. A psychiatrist told him he had both patricidal and matricidal tendencies. At age 18 Paul was diagnosed with a learning disorder called dysgraphia (difficulty in spelling), but the alleged damage to his psyche was already done. At one point he supposedly attempted suicide, using Tylenol and booze.

The childhood of Paul Cox became a motive for murder. The prosecution made much of the fact he had once threatened his brother with a knife during a tussle. Defense Counsel Rubin elicited testimony about childhood slights and scoldings in an effort to prove Cox was temporarily insane when he murdered his "parents," really the Drs. Chervu.

Perhaps most damning were Paul's own words. Prosecutor Bolen put four witnesses on the stand, all fellow members of Alcoholic Anonymous, to testify that he told them about dreams he had of entering the murder house and going upstairs. He even dreamed his hand moved in a stabbing or slashing motion.

Finally, Paul Cox took the stand at his second trial and admitted his guilt. He had no memory of the murders, but because of his dreams and after seeing the police evidence, he had come to believe he had done the deed. Because he could not remember, he must have been out of his mind, temporarily insane.

As was pointed out earlier, two juries had a hard time with the motive. The first trial resulted in a hung jury. After seven days of arguing, a single woman remained unconvinced and held out. In the second trial the jury deliberated for eight days, then rejected the murder charge and convicted Cox of manslaughter.

The difficulty the second jury had in reaching a verdict is not hard to understand. The state's case was surely weak. No murder weapon was ever found. No witnesses to the murders existed. No person could place Paul Cox at the Chervu house.

There was fingerprint evidence. An FBI agent testified that

a bloody handprint on the pillowcase next to Shanta Chervu's head belonged to Cox. Larchmont detectives were unable to ID the print for over four years, even though Cox had been in the Air Force and fingerprinted. And, the existence of the palm print means Cox was in the house, not necessarily that he killed anyone.

Cox's alleged motive–belief he was killing his parents–had to have been a stretch for the jury. If he had such thoughts, why act on them this night, among many nights, and in the wrong home?

Yet, Paul Cox, on the stand in his own defense, testified that although he had no memory of the murders, he believed he had done them. With that statement, the jury, unconvinced he had been temporarily insane, had to convict him of something. They elected for manslaughter.

Both prosecution and defense admitted that Paul Cox had blacked out and did not remember the events of that night. The defense put on Dr. David Weber to explain what a blackout was.

Dr. Weber said that in a blackout the "neurological, chemical processes by which we form permanent memory stops operating." Then he proceeded to get it polarly wrong. "A person in a blackout still has short-term memory..." he said.

The expert witness was correct in saying the person in a blackout "can still retrieve memories that he has previously made..." Then he contradicts himself in these words: "A person in a blackout might not be able to tell you who he is, might not be able to tell you when he first arrived in that city, might not be able to tell you what happened to him ten years ago."

In a word, that is expert nonsense.

Cox's blackout was well documented by Dr. Weber and others. On the evening of December 30 and into the early hours of December 31, Paul Cox and his best buddy, Gene Kelly, were at Gary's Barley Corn, a New Rochelle pub. Along with beer Cox consumed perhaps as many as a half dozen pitchers of kamikazes, a strong drink made of vodka, Triple Sec and lime juice.

Cox and Kelly decided to leave the bar. They piled into the front seat of Cox's car, really his mother's Chevrolet Impala. A third friend sat in back. A quarter mile up the road, they approached a sharp turn at Fifth Ave. and Slocum St. in Larchmont. Kelly said, "You're not going to make it."

That is the last thing Cox remembers until the next morning when his mother awoke him in his bed. Gene Kelly testified at the trial that the car crashed into a guardrail, jamming Kelly's door shut. While Kelly cursed him, Cox sat gripping the steering wheel, staring straight ahead, "like trying to figure out what he was going to do next."

According to Kelly, Cox now said, "I'm getting out of here." He opened the car door, got out and began walking toward his home. Kelly and the other man returned to Gary's Barley Corn for more drinks.

If the jury had heard testimony about blackouts, they would have learned that from the moment he heard Kelly's shouted warning, Cox stopped forming memory. His knowledge of the accident, any thought he might have had about what to do next, his words about getting out of there, his exiting the car and walking away would remain with him only moments, no longer than a minute or two.

By the time Paul Cox had traversed a half block, say a hundred yards at most, he would not remember the accident or where he was or where he was going. He would just be a seriously inebriated and unconscious young man walking somewhere unknown to him.

No one saw him, at least no one who has come forward. No one, including Cox, knows where he went and what he did on that walk. He could have gone anywhere, done anything. Until he awoke the next morning, Paul Cox was a person unable to learn, decide, form intent, consider consequences, reason. He was unconscious.

Two things are known about those few hours when Paul Cox was blacked out. Somehow he got home and into his own bed alone, actions his intact procedural memory enabled him to perform. Cox was also in the Chervu home. We know that, because his handprint was found on the bloody pillow of the bed where the couple lay dead.

The Chervu house was about a half mile from the accident scene, the Cox home about two miles. Therefore, it is possible that Cox went to the murder house before going home.

Why would he go there? He could not form intent, so it must be assumed he accidentally walked by the house. His long-term memory would enable him to recognize it as the place he had lived prior to age seven.

We know for a fact that he was in the house. Keeping in mind he could not form intent or decide anything, how might he have gotten inside? Only guesses are possible. He may have met someone on the street who led him inside or forced him to enter. He may have mistaken it for his current residence and entered, wanting to lie down and go to sleep, both instinctive acts requiring no thought.

The jury never heard it, but it is at least arguable that Paul Cox did the latter. He went to the rear of the house, just as he often did as a child. But the door was locked. The prosecution maintained that Cox broke a window, opened the door and entered the kitchen.

If the jury had heard testimony about blackouts, they might

have questioned (the defense certainly should have) whether a person in a blackout could have broken the window. It meant finding and picking up something to break the window with or using a padded elbow so as not to be cut, then reaching inside, finding the lock, unlocking and opening the door. All these are purposeful acts, involving planning, deliberation and intent–all of which the blacked out person is incapable of.

When I interviewed Cox in prison in August 2003, he provided additional information about the window. If true, the chances of a blacked out person entering the house through it become even more remote. (It may help in evaluating his information if I point out here that at the time Cox did not know the true nature of blackouts and could not have fudged his facts.)

In a written reply to a question from me, Cox said, "Next to the small screened-in porch, where the back door was located, there was a double-hung window. The screen from this window was found in the middle of the back yard. Along with the screen there was also a broom found in the vicinity. The DA put forth the idea that the broom was used to pry off the screen and then both were thrown into the yard. No fingerprints were found on the broom handle or the screen frame. He (the DA) was trying to show a conscious pattern of attempting to gain entry into the house. First the window, then the door."

Cox said that "this little piece of evidence" about the screen "completely confused my lawyer and I (sic)."

Given his blacked out state, it is extremely difficult to believe that Cox could have found a broom, pried off a screen, thrown both away, broken a window without being cut, reached inside and opened the door to enter the kitchen–and wiped his fingerprints off everything. This is a series of deliberate actions difficult for even a sober person. Even if he started the series of actions, he would not remember the task halfway through it.

The defense lawyer might at least have argued that Paul Cox–in a drunken state, let alone blacked out–could not have broken the window. To get inside the Chervu house he either had to have found the door already open or met someone who led or forced him inside.

Prosecutor Bolen made another argument to the jury. He said Cox went to the Chervu house by mistake all right, but he intended parenticide. He was bent, supposedly, on murdering Frank and Mary Cox. The simple fact is that a *blacked out Paul Cox or anyone else is incapable of forming intent to do anything beyond the instinctive.*

The prosecution also maintained that Cox picked up a large butcher knife when he entered the kitchen. It is possible to think of a way in which mindless, unconscious Cox might have done that. The kitchen had been remodeled since he was a boy. Lost, stumbling around in the dark, Cox's hand might have accidentally come across and picked up a knife. It's possible he might have become frightened and picked up a knife intuitively for protection. But if he did, he would in moments forget why he held it and drop it. He certainly did not deliberately "select" it from a rack.

Another possibility is that Cox, carrying the knife for some reason, goes upstairs to his old bedroom, awakens the Chervus, who scream and frighten him. Cox slashes with the knife, killing both.

Prosecutor Bolen theorized at one point that Mrs. Chervu heard noises, came downstairs and confronted a knife-wielding Cox. She screamed and ran upstairs to her husband. Cox followed and killed both. Maybe, but the problem is that by the time Cox reaches the top of the stairs he is not going to remember what he came for.

The greatest difficulty with either of these scenarios is trying to imagine a drunken, blacked out, unconscious and zombie-like

Cox murdering these two people. It is extremely difficult for even a strong, healthy, conscious and sober man to kill two people with a knife. This was one of the problems in the O. J. Simpson case. Dr. Lakshman Rao Chervu, a radiochemist, was 58, his wife Shanta, a geriatric physician, was 51. Both were in good health, capable of defending themselves.

Yet, the husband, still under the bed covers, was stabbed 15 times–in the face, neck, hand, lung, liver, pancreas, stomach, intestines and kidneys. The wife, lying perpendicular to him, her head on his arm, her feet touching the floor, was stabbed nine times–in the chest, upper arm, heart, lung, esophagus and abdominal organs. Both had their throats cut. Blood covered the bed, walls and ceiling of the room. A more grisly, ghastly scene is hard to imagine.

A total of 24 stab wounds were inflicted. Especially if one or both of the Chervus were struggling with him, the assault had to take some minutes of frantic stabbing. If the assailant were someone in a blackout, he might wield a knife. But 24 times? Somewhere in the middle of it, he would forget what he's doing, drop the knife and walk away.

The murders went undiscovered for 36 hours. The couple's daughter, Arati Chervu Johnston, who lived in Canada, phoned her parents on New Year's eve and the following morning, but got no answer. Worried, she phoned her uncle, Narayan Basetti, in Flushing, N. Y. He phoned the New Rochelle Hospital emergency room, learning Dr. Shanta had not showed up for work on the 1 p.m. shift.

Acting on an uneasy feeling, Basetti drove to his sister's house. When he discovered the broken pane of glass in the rear door he "literally ran" to his car and drove to the police station. Sgt. Kenneth Kahn of the Larchmont police was the first to ascend the stairs and find the bodies. The lights were on in the house.

When the killer left, he took the murder weapon with him, hiding it so that it was never found, despite a thorough search. Police also believed the killer would've been covered in blood. They looked for bloody clothing, but found none.

If Paul Cox or anyone in a blackout did somehow and for some reason murder this couple, it is impossible to believe he could hide the murder weapon and clothing so they were never found. A blacked out Cox wouldn't remember that he even committed a murder for more than a minute. He will certainly be unaware he needs to cover up or hide anything. He won't be able to form any intent or to carry it out. A person in a blackout, such as Cox, would simply walk away, perhaps ending up at home and in bed, as he did.

Paul Cox awoke the next morning, naked, unable to find his black jeans, white shirt and new sneakers, all Christmas gifts, he had worn the evening before. Also missing was the Navy pea coat he'd worn for warmth. He never did find them. His mother swore on the stand she hadn't either.

In my prison interview with Cox, I asked him about his car keys and wallet–questions he said no one had ever asked him before. He said he retrieved his keys the next morning, when he and his mother went to the police station to pick up the car. If he had no keys, how did he get into his home? He replied that there was entry through the garage, which the whole family used.

Was his wallet missing? Cox said he never had to replace his driver's license and such, so he must not have lost it. Yet, he had no recollection of either losing or finding it. Cox said he disliked carrying a wallet, preferring to put his money in his pocket. When driving he would often place his wallet on the dashboard or in the glove compartment. His guess is that he either left the wallet at home when he went out or the police found it and returned it to him the next day.

If Cox had murdered the Chervus while in his blackout, he would not have realized the need to get rid of his bloody clothes. He might have realized the bloody clothes were wet and uncomfortable and removed them. But all of them, including underwear, shoes and socks? And if he did, he would have dropped them where he stood. He would never have formulated the need to hide them. Why would he? He doesn't remember murdering anyone. And who would consider this mindless drunk capable of hiding anything so it was never found? After all a blacked out person doesn't even know enough to come in out of the rain.

If Paul Cox is the murderer, he had to have removed his clothes, gotten rid of them, then walked home naked, in the wee hours of a cold winter night, remembering none of it.

The nakedness and missing attire are facts. We need to consider them. What are the circumstances in which a grown man disrobes, down to his wherewithal? He does so to take a bath or shower; to go to bed; to change his clothing; to go swimming (although something might be worn); or because he fell in some water, mud or other substance and became wet.

Another reason comes to mind. A man might disrobe because someone else forced him to, someone wearing bloody clothes who wanted to steal clean ones, someone who knew a naked man would not easily go for help.

They never did, but it seems to me the defense team for Paul Cox might have raised reasonable doubt if they had possessed some elementary knowledge of blackouts. For example, they could have offered a scenario in which Cox comes to the rear of the house, finds it already broken into and the door open, and is confronted by a man wearing bloody clothes and wielding a bloody knife, who demands he take off his clothes and give them to him.

Why didn't he simply kill Cox and steal his clothes? He wanted them clean, not bloody from another murder. Why not kill the naked Cox? He didn't for some reason. Perhaps he was in a hurry to get out of there. If the real murderer went by car, the missing knife and clothes are long gone.

In my interview and in his follow up letter to me, Cox provided additional information. He said his own DNA was retrieved from a small drop of blood found on a Venetian blind cord that hung on the back door to the house. Where Cox's blood came from, when there is no evidence he was cut and bleeding, remains a mystery.

Adding to the mystery is Cox's statement that DNA of unknown origin was located just inside the back door in the kitchen. A mystery fingerprint was also found on the sash of the broken window. Cox said his own fingerprint was also found in the kitchen.

If true, this DNA and fingerprint evidence is surely puzzling. At the very least, it suggests that Paul Cox may not have been alone in the kitchen the night of the murders. The jury might well have wanted to learn this.

In any event, a naked, confused Cox stands there, perhaps in the kitchen, after the murderer leaves, then wanders upstairs, finds the bodies and leaves his handprint as he leans over them to see who they are. Then he walks home and goes to bed.

This is pure guesswork on my part. There may not be a word of truth to it. But it is at least as plausible as the prosecution's farfetched scheme of mistaken parenticide. But Defense Counsel Rubin knew nothing about blackouts. The jurors reached a verdict, never possessing full information about the case.

Paul Cox knew nothing about blackouts either, although he'd had lots of them. He confessed to having murdered the Drs. Chervu, even though it was doubtful, unlikely and even impossible for him to have done so, at least as the prosecution maintained he did.

On the day of his conviction, Frank Cox, Paul's father, arose to formally apologize to the Chervu family for what his son had done.

On March 14, 1995 the day of his sentencing to two consecutive terms of 16 and 2/3 to 50 years in prison, Paul Cox faced the Chervu family and said, "I am remorseful. I am sorry. If there was something I could do or say, I would.... For the rest of my life, I am going to regret what happened that night." He tried to go on, but broke down. His attorney finished his statement

How on earth did Paul Cox come to confess to a crime he doesn't remember doing? We take this up next.

13
Only In His Dreams

The Chervu murders were a sensation in Larchmont and other towns of Westchester County. *The New York Times* gave it extensive coverage, something it seldom does with murders.

Few people were more interested than Frank and Mary Cox. They knew the Chervus, in fact had sold their old home to them 14 years before. The Coxes devoured news stories and video taped TV newscasts. The murders and search for the killers were dinner table conversation.

Living at home, the 21-year-old Paul Cox absorbed all this, but kept his mouth shut about the fear that gripped him. He alone knew he had blacked out the night of the murders, indeed had no memory of what he might have done during the time the sleeping couple were slain. And what had happened to the clothes he wore that night?

This was something more than an idle worry to Paul Cox. Not knowing the next morning what happened or what was said the night before is diabolical. All of us take for granted our memory of events, our ability to monitor and censor our actions. It assures us we were and are okay. We did nothing wrong or we can make right what we did wrong. To not know is terrifying, especially when guilt over getting drunk and blacking out is layered on top.

No better example of this is Henry M. He lives a protected life in a home, constantly supervised. Even after decades without memory formation, Henry constantly worries about what he might have just said or done. A dozen times a day he asks what he just said or did and needs reassurance that he did nothing wrong.

Paul Cox was Henry M. greatly magnified. But where was his reassurance?

Cox began to dream that he entered his childhood home, walked around the kitchen, then went upstairs, turned left into his old room and found a couple lying in bed. They were faceless. And he said or did nothing to them. They were just there. In his dreams, the house was as it had been in his childhood, the old kitchen, not the remodeled one. A green carpet, since replaced, still covered the stairs.

Dreaming about former residences is pretty common stuff. Perhaps the only people who don't have such dreams never moved. But most people have not had a loss of memory about a period when a savage double murder was committed–or the guilt associated with it.

Something else was working on Paul Cox. He had a learning disorder that went undiagnosed until he was age 18. His spelling was atrocious. His grade card looked like a study in fourth and fifth letters of the alphabet–entirely unacceptable in the Cox family.

For most of his life, Cox was disapproved of and scolded, then sent to a succession of psychologists and psychiatrists to diagnose what was wrong with him. One, who shall be nameless here (lest someone else go to him), told the young man he had patricidal and matricidal, if not suicidal, tendencies. One good thing: at least he did not urge a lobotomy.

A failure at school and everything he tried, including a brief stint in the Air Force, Cox became a secret and serious drinker. He took pride in his ability to drive while drunk. Never had an accident, until he hit the guardrail at Fifth and Slocum.His downward spiral of drink and drift continued until November 1990, almost two years after the murders, when his then girlfriend convinced him to join Alcoholics Anonymous (AA). She testified at his trial under the name Miss S.

Formed in 1935 in Akron, Ohio, by Bill W. and Dr. Bob, AA has more than 100,000 groups with 2.1 million members in 146 countries. As such it is the foremost organization dealing with alcoholism. Its techniques are now used in treatment of drug abuse, gambling, overeating and other problems. The AA techniques, largely developed by Bill W., may be said to have revolutionized psychology, psychiatry and addictive medicine.

AA describes itself this way: "Alcoholics Anonymous is a fellowship of men and women who share their experience, strength and hope with each other that they may solve their common problem and help others to recover from alcoholism. The only requirement for membership is a desire to stop drinking. There are no dues or fees for AA membership; we are self-supporting through our own contributions. AA is not allied with any sect, denomination, politics, organization or institution; does not wish to engage in any controversy; neither endorses nor opposes any causes. Our primary purpose is to stay sober and help other alcoholics to achieve sobriety."

The key word in AA is *anonymous*. The member has no identity other than a first name, and the fact of membership is not known to anyone outside the organization. Anything said at an AA meeting remains confidential among those who heard it and is not to be shared with anyone not in attendance. The purpose of this anonymity is to remove the social stigma associated with alcoholism so the member can speak freely about his addiction, learn he is not alone, and get help from fellow members.

As developed by Bill W., AA practices a Twelve Step program of spiritual awakening, in which the aid of a God or Supreme Being is enlisted to help cure alcoholism.

It was Steps 4 and 5 that caused a problem for Paul Cox. Putting the two steps together, the AA members "made a searching and fearless moral inventory of ourselves; admitted to God, to ourselves, and to another human being the exact nature of our wrongs."

The idea behind these steps is for the member to bring out into the open and deal with those guilty secrets that might someday cause him to relapse into drinking. Paul Cox believed he had a powerfully big secret.

Miss S. testified that Paul "got very upset and he asked me if I remembered the murders that happened in Larchmont a few years earlier." She said he told her, "I don't remember this night. I don't know what went on and I'm afraid I might have done it." Miss S. said she told him, "Paul, I think I know you almost better than anybody–there is no way that you could have done it."

Cox told his AA sponsor, a Mr. C. about his blackout and the murders. Mr. C. took it up with a senior member of the AA group, a Mr. O., who advised Cox to seek therapy and hire an attorney. Another AA member gave Cox the best advice. In essence, he told him to seek therapy, continue attending meetings, but keep his mouth shut about the murders.

But Cox couldn't stop talking about them. He continued to bring up his fears at AA meetings. At some point he and some other AA members began to share an apartment. The arrangement was a great aid to sobriety, but it only worsened Cox's fixation on the murders. The roommates, joined by other AA members, kept on trying to figure out how Cox might have done the murders. Where did he get the knife? What did he do with it? What happened to his bloody clothes? Why did he go into the house? Why did he kill the Chervus? How did he get home naked?

The answers to these questions became evident at the trial. Mr. O. said he saw Cox after he'd been in therapy a few weeks and Paul said "his memory was cleared up. He couldn't really handle it at the time when we first spoke, but he had in fact committed the crime."

Miss S., Cox's old girlfriend, said Cox told her he'd found a knife the morning after the murders and thrown it into the Long Island Sound off Manor Park. Cox told her the knife had blood on it, but she reminded herself that Cox sometimes cut himself intentionally. Once he had cut the letters H-E-L-P into his arm, she said.

A Mr. S. said Cox told him "he had gone into a house in New Rochelle and had killed two people there while they slept–that was the skinny of it." Another AA member said Cox drove by the house where it happened the next day." Mr. C. testified that Cox told him "his mother had thrown the bloody clothes away."

A Mr. R., one of Cox's roommates, said Cox told him he didn't know why he grabbed the knife. He wandered through the house and wound up in the master bedroom and sat down on the edge of the bed. Mr. R. testified, "The woman woke up, and he stabbed her many times. He told me the man woke up and was pleading with him, and he stabbed him many times, and that before he left, he slit their throats to make sure they were dead, and then he fled." He described Cox's recollections as "clear as a bell."

Miss H. told the court she was contemplating moving into the Cox apartment when he told her that he sometimes woke up screaming in the middle of the night from dreams that he had murdered two people in an alcohol blackout. He told her he remembered going to the house, breaking the windowpane, then coming back early the next morning to try to clean up the fingerprints. Nonetheless, she moved in with Cox.

This sort of lurid testimony from Cox's fellow AA members began his trial. It surely impressed the audience and doubtlessly the jury, but someone should have questioned it. The positions of the bodies–the husband on his back still under the covers, the wife sideways on the bed, her head on her husband's arm, her feet on the floor–raised issues about the order of the killings. One cannot help but wonder if Cox really did sit on the side of the bed, chat with Mrs. Chervu, then stab her nine times, after which her husband woke up and pleaded with Cox before being stabbed 15 times.

And there was no testimony to support Cox's statements that he remembered going to the house and breaking the window, or about returning to the murder house and wiping away fingerprints and other evidence. It sounds made up, doesn't it?

Finally, there was Mary Cox's testimony that she never found any bloody clothing in her son's bedroom or anywhere else.

The prosecution saw the testimony from AA members as corroboration that Cox really did remember what happened and what he did that murder night. But it was at least arguable (and no one did) that Cox, egged on by his buddies, is engaging in increasingly desperate efforts to explain his dreams. Over the years the dreams progressed to the point where Cox felt a slashing or stabbing motion in his right hand as he looked at them. The faces were now his parents.

Finally, in January 1993, four years after the murders and two years after Cox initially confessed to AA members, Miss H. told the police about Cox's statements. Cox was eventually arrested on May 20, 1993, held for three weeks, then released on $250,000 bond. He was to wear an electronic monitor on his ankle and live at his parents' home. That's right. The same Frank and Mary Cox he was accused of attempting to kill when he mistakenly stabbed the Chervus.

Cox did not testify at his first trial. The only knowledge of his confession came from AA members. This trial resulted in a hung jury, one woman remaining unconvinced.

At his second trial, Cox took the stand and confessed. He said that when the police showed him their evidence against him, he became convinced he had committed murders he did not remember doing. He admitted to a sense of relief that his ordeal of doubt was over.

Other than the finger and hand print, and DNA perhaps, the police had no other evidence linking Cox to the crimes–and the prints proved only that he was there, not that he committed the murders.

A practitioner of Freudian theory would argue that Paul Cox couldn't remember the murders because the deed was so horrible his mind repressed it to protect itself from such terrible knowledge. Perhaps, but Paul Cox's memory loss is total, from just before the accident until the next morning. If he repressed the murders, he still ought to remember the accident, walking, entering his home, going to bed or other happenings not associated with the Chervu house.

The suddenness and totality of the memory loss suggests he never formed any memory of any kind during the blackout brought on by alcohol.

It never happened, but it was at least possible to argue at Cox's trial that his confession was false, more imagination and guesswork than fact. Here was a young man, highly impressionable, an underachiever, a failure at almost everything he tried, scolded, probed by shrinks who tell him he's dangerous to others and essentially worthless. He takes up drink. He must be considered an alcoholic.

Now comes the blackout. Under the best of circumstances not remembering causes worry and guilt. But Cox's fears are greatly magnified by the fact two people were murdered in his old bedroom during the period he can't remember. His doubts and worries consume him. He begins to dream.

Again no one did, but someone might have pointed out at Cox's trial that it is impossible to dream about something unknown. A person cannot dream in a foreign language unless they know that language. He may add or subtract in his dream, but he will not perform calculus unless he has such knowledge. A person may dream of an unknown place, such as a foreign country, but it is populated with familiar sights and people.

Paul Cox always dreamed of the Chervu house as it had been when he was seven, including furniture. He never dreamed of a remodeled kitchen or new carpeting on the stairs. If he came to kill his parents, wouldn't he have turned right at the top of the stairs to their old room, rather than left to his old room, now the master bedroom? If he had been in the house, wouldn't his dreams reflect recent knowledge?

We have a young, suggestible, guilt-ridden, unstable and alcoholic young man. Now put him in an environment in which he is encouraged, for his own recovery, to make a "searching and fearless moral inventory" of his sins, then admit to God, himself and other people the "exact nature" of his "wrongs." Anything revealed will remain confidential, of course.

This is powerful stuff for the strongest-willed person. For someone like Paul Cox it was positively incendiary. Did he ever have a "wrong" to make an "inventory" of! And, because he couldn't remember, Cox and his AA buddies tried to determine the "exact nature" of how he murdered two people. Cox became convinced.

So did everyone else involved in the case.

Cox was tried in 1994. By that time, surely, someone had heard of false memories, much discussed at the time. Much publicity had been given to cases in which people "remembered" things that simply had never happened, such as childhood molestations.

Psychological literature contained many studies in which memories were altered or entirely falsified as a result of suggestive or leading questions. To cite one of many, subjects were shown fake photographs of themselves enjoying a balloon ride as a child–a ride that never occurred. Nonetheless, fully half the subjects recalled the ride and picture being taken. The bottom line is that no one's memories are entirely trustworthy.

And Paul Cox's memory was even more suspect. In truth, he had no memory for the time of the murders. Could he be allowing himself to be convinced he had done something he had no personal knowledge of and never would?

Detectives are familiar with false confessions. Mentally deranged people who come forth insisting they did the deed plague every major crime. Police routinely keep private some piece of evidence that only the killer would know, as a test against false confessions. Detectives have learned not to carelessly question witnesses for fear they may taint actual memories by suggestion of what happened. It is better to leave the witness alone, so memories remain intact for accurate recall later.

Isn't it just a little surprising that no one, not Cox, not his father, none of his AA friends, no experts cast a shred of doubt on the authenticity of Cox's confession? Defense attorney Rubin put all his eggs in the temporary insanity basket. When the basket did not hold up, no eggs were left.

Paul Cox may well be guilty, but the jurors might feel better about it today had they heard expert testimony about false memory and false confession, at the very least heard from someone casting doubt on Cox's admitted role.

One more time, I am not arguing the innocence of Paul Cox. I don't know, he may be guilty of the murders. What I do know is that failure to consider recent information about alcohol blackouts–available at the time of his trial–gives the appearance of injustice if not actual injustice.

One thing is certain. Paul Cox may be one of the few people ever convicted on the basis of dreams. It may be said he dreamed himself into prison.

His prison is no dream. In early August 2003, I spent six hours there interviewing Cox for this book. It is a highly unpleasant, most depressing place. I couldn't wait to leave.

At the time Cox was eight years into his sentence. He married before going to prison and is a father. My biggest impression of him was his size. He is slender, slight of build and no taller than I. Trying to imagine him struggling with and managing to murder two people with a knife is difficult.

We need to consider one other question briefly. Did the usually mild-mannered Paul Cox turn into Mr. Hyde during his blackout, flailing away 24 times with a knife, killing two innocent people he didn't know?

The prosecution tried to prove he might have by describing a childhood incident in which Cox held a knife at the throat of his brother during a tussle. It really doesn't look like much more than a sibling spat, but even exaggerating it's significance hardly makes Cox a violent person.

Despite many drunken episodes and a great deal of tension with his parents and teachers, Cox had no record of violence or other assaults. Michael Newbury, Gene Fekete and the others who murdered in a blackout had a history of assaults and other violence while drinking.

Perhaps there is a first time for everything, but Cox's whole life suggests a Dr. Jekyll, not a Mr. Hyde.

Paul Cox's attorney appealed his conviction on the grounds that the judge had improperly allowed AA members to testify about what Cox had said to them in confidence. A U.S. District judge agreed with this, in effect affording AA the same status as organized religion. The U. S. Court of Appeals and finally the U. S. Supreme Court reversed this decision.

In my opinion this was the correct ruling. AA itself has never claimed or sought a religious status. AA members are not asked to confess to possible criminal acts. Instead, they are urged to talk to lawyers and therapists.

14
Throw Away The Key

The law recognizes that the alcohol blackout occurs, all right. But it doesn't matter or make any difference. Under the law, the blackout is just a stage of drinking, and if a person drinks, he is responsible for his actions.

If he gets into a bar fight; drives the interstate and burns up five people in a car crash; murders his girlfriend in a rage; enters his old home and kills two people sleeping there; if he does any of myriad other crimes, then he is responsible for his actions and must pay the price. Lock him up and throw away the key.

There is a point of view that applauds this. A person should be held accountable for his actions under the law and appropriately punished. I cannot disagree. I do not believe I have a liberal bone in my body. A bleeding heart coddler of miscreants is the last thing I am. If incarceration will prevent crime, then I'm all for it.

Yet, the question must be asked: what is appropriate punishment? Under our system of jurisprudence, judges and juries are stuck with the answer–and it is no easy task. Throwing away the key may be a relatively easy decision when dealing with a hardened criminal or a sadistic spree killer. But these are a small minority of the millions of people in our prisons and jails.

In meting out punishment, the law affords special status to

juveniles and first offenders. Courts take into consideration such states as diminished capacity, mental illness, temporary insanity and irresistible impulse in determining guilt and punishment. We all know of much-publicized cases in which admitted perpetrators received reduced sentences or got off entirely because of childhood deprivation or abuse, spousal battery and parental cruelty.

However, in determining guilt and punishment, the law does not recognize the diminished capacities stemming from the interruption of working memory during an alcohol blackout.

The law would not dream of locking up Henry M. because he cannot remember anything long enough to know what he's doing. The man is considered incapacitated and institutionalized, constantly supervised. If he got out and performed some crime, the law would punish those responsible for his care, not Henry.

Yet, the law locks up Kevin Price, Paul Cox and others like them for a temporary similarity to Henry M. While they are blacked out, they are no more conscious and in control of their faculties than Henry. Yet, the key is thrown away.

Perhaps worse, no differentiation is made between the person with a history of blackouts who continues to drink and the moderate or naïve drinker having his first blackout experience.

I am not a lawyer. I know I am invading the turf of those expert in the law. But it is not difficult to think of several legal issues involved in blackouts.

- Can a person be held responsible for his actions while in an unconscious state?
- If a person does not know where he or she is, what time it is, where she is going, what she is saying or doing; if the person cannot remember anything beyond a moment, cannot learn, form intent or make a plan is she responsible for what she

does?

- What is the responsibility of the persons who provided him the alcohol or failed to recognize his impulsive, unconscious state and keep him from harming himself and others?
- Can a person confess to actions he does not remember? Can a person even take the stand and testify about events that occurred while he or she was blacked out?
- Is justice served when the law declares that if a person chooses to drink he is responsible for all that happens thereafter, even if he doesn't remember it? And, if so, should there be warning labels on cans and bottles and signs posted in bars warning about the risks of blackouts, especially if one drinks too fast on an empty stomach?

I realize these questions open up a can of worms for lawyers and judges. I'm sorry, but I have no answers to offer.

I am wholly sympathetic to the truly gargantuan tasks police officers face in coping with crime and protecting the public. I hate to add to their burden, but the new knowledge about blackouts makes it necessary.

The police problem with blackouts may be illustrated by the case of Gary Gauger.

Morris and Ruth Gauger were murdered on April 8, 1993 at their farm in McHenry County, Illinois. The couple operated a motorcycle shop and sold imported rugs in addition to farming. Their son, Gary Gauger, who lived with them, discovered the body of his father, aged 74, the next day. He called paramedics who notified the sheriff. Shortly after the deputies arrived, they found the body of Ruth Gauger, 70, in a trailer where she sold rugs.

Gary Gauger, 41, was taken into custody. After an allnight interrogation, he was said to have made statements that police and prosecutors claimed constituted a confession. Gauger said he had been drinking and blacked out. He knew nothing of the killings. Gauger further insisted that he had made the statements to deputies only hypothetically after they persuaded him it was possible he had committed the murders during an alcohol blackout. The statement was not recorded and there was no contemporaneous record of it.

Gauger went on trial in May 1993, charged with two counts of murder. There was no physical evidence linking him to the crime. The alleged confession was the state's entire case.

At a hearing on a pretrial motion to suppress the confession, Gauger testified that deputies had induced him to speculate about how he might have committed the crime. He said they told him he had failed a polygraph test and his clothes, drenched in blood were found in his room. In truth, the polygraph had been inconclusive and there were no bloody clothes.

At the trial, deputies said Gauger told them he committed the crimes by coming upon his parents from behind, pulling their heads back by their hair and cutting their throats. A pathologist and forensic scientist both testified that the victims' wounds and hairs found at the scene were consistent with the alleged confession.

The jury found Gauger guilty on both counts. He waived a jury for sentencing and Judge Henry L. Cowlin sentenced him to death on January 11, 1994. The sentence was later reduced to life in prison.

On March 8, 1996, the Illinois appellate court unanimously reversed the decision and remanded the case for a new trial on the grounds Judge Cowlin erred in failing to grant the motion to suppress Gauger's alleged confession. In an unpublished opinion, two judges held that the statements were the fruit of an arrest made without probable cause and therefore should not have been admitted at the trial.

Without the confession, State's Attorney Gary W. Pack had no other evidence and had to drop the charges. But Pack and deputies continued to insist Gauger had in fact committed the crimes, but without the confession, they could not prove it.

Thus it remained until June 1997, when a federal grand jury in Milwaukee indicted two members of a Wisconsin motorcycle gang, known as the Outlaws, for 34 acts of racketeering, including murder of the Gaugers. One Outlaw, James Schneider, pleaded guilty to acts relating to the murders. Another, Randall E. Miller, was convicted in federal court in June 2000.

After his release Gauger returned to farming in McHenry County. "Until this happened," he said, "I really believed in the criminal justice system."

The interrogation of Gauger was merely typical of that performed by police all over the country. It is depicted on many "cop shows" on TV. Using the "good cop-bad cop" technique, detective seek to both intimidate and befriend the suspect, hoping he will confess. It is lawful for detectives to falsify information about the investigation. They may tell a suspect they have polygraph results, bloody clothes, fingerprints on a murder weapon, irrefutable DNA evidence, eyewitnesses who saw him do it when they don't. If that discourages the suspect and leads him to confess his involvement in the crime, then the lies are merely good police work.

But few would argue, in hindsight, that the fraudulent confession obtained from Gary Gauger was good police work.

Far be it from me to tell the police how to do their jobs, but they may want to realize just how vulnerable the person is after a blackout. Some hours or days in his life are a blank. He has no knowledge of what happened. That is unnerving and he is full of guilt for not remembering. He is desperate to fill in the void.

This man is easy pickings for any halfway glib person who can weave a plausible tale about what might have happened. Gauger's parents were dead, and he had no memory of anything. No special talent was required to concoct a convincing tale of how and why he might have killed them. Two people were murdered in the house where Paul Cox formerly dwelled. It was not hard to think of a convincing tale by which he might have mistakenly slain them.

If making arrests and obtaining convictions are the prime goal, then a suspect who blacked out makes it easy. If truly solving crime, achieving justice and having convictions stand up on appeal are the goals, then the blackout should be taken seriously and the suspect treated carefully.

Unfortunately, the police and prosecutors sometimes face an opposite problem–suspects and defendants who make false claims of blackouts. The problem may be illustrated by a murder case that occurred in my hometown of Santa Barbara, California.

On May 14, 2000 Charles Watson Ford, aged 73, dialed 911 to report the murder of Ms. Jesus Belen Lopez, age 37. She was shot in the head at close range. Police came, took him to the station, where he described in detail how, while drunk, he murdered Ms. Lopez, because she refused to have sex with him and threatened to leave him.

At his trial in October 2003, Ford changed his story, claiming he was in an alcohol blackout at the time of the murder and remembers only fragments of the night. He remembers cooking bacon and eggs. He said he remembers sitting in a chair with the gun in his hand wondering why the gun was loaded. He testified, "...like somewhere in a far-off canyon, I can hear the weapon discharge." He remembers "only seconds" of his 40-minute 911 call. He said he has no memory of walking out of his house and surrendering to deputies, quite naked.

Readers of this book will already have spotted the falsity in

Ford's claim of memory loss. Remembering gun shots, calling 911, then confessing in detail how and why he committed the crime is utterly impossible for a blacked out person.

Senior District Attorney Joyce Dudley said two experts on blackouts testified at the trial. One said that Ford was blacked out, the other said that if he called 911 and confessed he was not. The jury believed the latter expert and convicted Ford of first-degree murder. Yet, it is the measure of the problem that the jury heard such contradictory testimony and had to decide who was correct.

Law enforcement and the courts desperately need to standardize what a blackout is. First, the police should understand the blacked out person did not forget. He never formed any memory for a time. This thrust him into an unconscious state in which he had no idea what he was doing or why. The police and prosecutors should realize he is incapable of intent at that stage. Even if he were caught at the scene, gun in hand, bodies all around, the most he can be charged with is manslaughter. He is incapable of planning and executing the murder.

Second, the police desperately need an official and recognized test to detect the person in a blackout. I believe a simple test of short-term memory, such as the word test described in Chapter Eight, will suffice. With such a test at his disposal the officer at a crime or accident scene would be able to say he administered the memory test and the suspect knew all the words. He was not blacked out. Or he knew only one word and was probably blacked out.

Third, the police need to be trained in how to determine if a blackout occurred after the fact. It is the next day. The suspect says he was blacked out and can't remember anything from the night before. Is he telling the truth or malingering?

In looking for an answer, the police should understand that

the blackout is total and the onset of the blackout is abrupt. He should have a last memory then draw a total blank until he remembers something hours later or whenever he recovers. Kevin Price was in a bathroom. His next memory is three days later in a hospital bed. Paul Cox heard the words, "You're not going to make it." His next memory is his mother awakening him the following morning.

There must be absolutely nothing in between. He cannot remember part of it, one thing but not another, as Charles Ford attempted to do in the above case. He cannot say he remembers sitting in a chair, holding a gun and hearing a shot. Never happen. A blacked out person remembers nothing. Even if a person with him truthfully tells him what happened, the blacked out person will not remember it.

It may be possible theoretically, but it is not easy to fake a blackout. It is on a par with pretending you don't understand a language when you do. An expression or reaction gives you away.

In evaluating the blackout, the person's memories should always be consistent. The last and first memories must remain the same forever, as they are with Paul Cox and Kevin Price. One cannot change stories, as Ford did. And, a blacked out person should have no knowledge of anything that happened to anyone in the world during the blackout. Repeated and careful questioning about events, both remembered and unremembered, should reveal to the police when a person is telling the truth or malingering about a blackout.

Or, the subject may be ordered to take the Symptom Validity Test (SVT). It was developed to detect false claims of amnesia, those "can't remembers" claimed in as many as 45 per cent of homicide cases. The suspect is asked to answer 15 to 100 true or false questions about a crime or event. Typical questions might be: Was a gun or knife used in the crime? Was the victim white or black? Were lights on in the building? Every question must be answered. If the person does not know, he is to guess at the answer.

If the person truly does not remember, random guessing will produce a score of about 50 per cent. Scores well above or below that mark indicate the person has knowledge of the crime and is trying to conceal it. Properly administered the SVT is virtually foolproof.

Fourth, if the police believe the suspect was in a blackout when he committed the crime, then they must consider his diminished capacities. He or she cannot remember anything for more than a moment or two. Chances are they don't know where they are or what day of the week or time it is. They cannot form intent, decide anything, or carry it out. Whatever crime they committed must be impulsive and of short duration.

Michael Newbury, Gene Fekete, James Edward Reid, Steven Schoff, Christopher Bailey and Robert Mark Edwards were alone with their victims and acted quickly. Gary Gauger and Paul Cox faced two people and needed a protracted period to kill them. It is simply difficult to believe a person unable to form memory could do this. One, maybe, but two? And with a knife?

It is not at all easy for the police or anyone to put themselves in the mind of a blacked out person. We take for granted that every person forms intent and decides something. We cannot imagine conduct sans intent. I've been observing people in blackouts it for years, but I only belatedly realized Cox could not have broken the window and reached inside to unlock the door. That is a deliberate action involving intent.

The police must ask themselves if such a debilitated person could have committed the crime in question? If they don't ask, sooner or later some defense lawyer will.

I began this chapter by asking what is suitable punishment for a person in a blackout who commits a crime?

I believe unequivocally that a person who commits violence while drinking, whether blacked out or not, must be prevented from ever drinking again. Counseling, some form of therapy, use of drugs such as antabuse, a prison sentence followed by prolonged probation, throwing away the key or some combination of these must be used to protect society.

I said it earlier, but it bears repeating: the man who beats women and children, drunk or sober, conscious or blacked out, has something seriously wrong with him. If his condition cannot be treated and cured, he should be prevented from drinking.

But what is suitable punishment for persons committing non-violent crimes while in a blackout? As horrible as Kevin Price's accident was, I felt his sentence of 21 years in prison to be excessive. He had never blacked out before and didn't even know it was possible. And he had no particular record for either violence or reckless driving. No intent or malice was involved in the accident.

I thought a shorter sentence followed by prolonged probation and supervision was more in order. That's pretty much what happened. Price served five years, then was put on probation for 10 more.

I also believe the Cox sentence to be excessive. The murders were ghastly, to be sure. Even if he did actually commit them, the fact of blackout removes any intent or deliberation. He had a long history of blackouts, but no history of violence during them. He had voluntarily quit drinking two years or more before his arrest.

At this writing, Cox has been in prison eight years. One must ask, how much is enough? When do society and the penal system begin to offer absolution?

15
A Promising Start

If blackouts are thought of at all in our society, it is as a subject of humor, the besotted drunk trying to figure out where he is and what happened. The late Foster Brooks made a career out of playing such a drunk (although he himself did not drink), and he was indeed hilarious.

If I have accomplished nothing else, I hope the reader accepts that the alcohol blackout is a serious condition. We have people walking around in an unconscious state–and driving and flying and performing other dangerous tasks. Something really ought to be done about it.

And little or nothing is.

The depth of the neglect may be understood by looking at the DSM-IV TR (Diagnostic and Statistical Manual, Fourth Edition). This thick tome is the diagnostic "bible" of psychiatry, used by physicians to identify psychiatric disorders.

The latest DSM-IV TR revisions mention blackouts–but barely. On Page 522, in discussing "differential diagnosis" of "dissociative amnesia (formerly Psychogenic Amnesia)," the following is written:

"Memory loss associated with *Substance Intoxication* (e.g. "Blackouts") can be distinguished from Dissociative Amnesia by the association of the memory loss with heavy substance use and the fact that the amnesia usually cannot be reversed."

Other passages might be quoted, but the bottom line is that psychiatrists are to identify blackouts as irreversible, the sort of permanent memory loss afflicting advanced alcoholics, notably those with Korsakov's Syndrome.

No recognition is given to the occurrence of blackouts to moderate, light and even first time drinkers; nor to the fact the blacked out person is functioning while unconscious; nor to ways to hopefully prevent the condition.

Apparently psychiatrists believe they do not have to concern themselves with the alcohol blackout because it is transient and the person recovers.

This might rank as a curiosity, except the various manifestations of alcoholism, indeed all of addiction medicine, are increasingly the province of psychiatry. If psychiatrists don't concern themselves with blackouts, who is going to?

It is as though one of the more common problems associated with alcohol is a secret. Why this is so baffles the mind. Every other manifestation of alcoholism has been studied in the extreme, written about, discussed and lectured on. I can only guess that both writers and speakers figured loss of memory was just something that happened to people who drank to excess. Solution to the problem was easy. Just drink less. End of subject.

The alcohol blackout has fallen through the cracks of medicine. We need to discover how that happened before we can consider what to do about it.

The first serious study of blackouts was reported in 1946 by E. M. Jellinek. He questioned members of Alcoholics Anonymous and formulated his concept of phases of drinking history among alcoholics. But his major contribution, no small one indeed, was to identify alcoholism as a disease. It surely is that.

In the late 1960s and early 1970s–more than thirty years ago at this writing–Donald W. Goodwin, M. D., a psychiatrist, began to study alcohol blackouts while on the faculty of the Washington University, School of Medicine, in St. Louis, Missouri. Most of what we know about blackouts comes from the work of Dr. Goodwin and a handful of others. As with most pioneer research, his work raises as many questions as it answers. Regrettably, the work that began with such promise was soon abandoned.

In 1969, Goodwin and his associates interviewed 100 hospitalized alcoholics about their experiences with memory loss. Goodwin found that 64 members of his group reported having experienced memory loss while drinking. They said this generally first occurred midway or late in the course of alcoholism and almost never after only moderate drinking.

From his study, Goodwin concluded there are two types of blackouts. One he called *en bloc*, the person has no memory after a given moment. The second type of memory loss Goodwin called fragmentary. The person remembers only part of an event and may remember a little more if prodded or reminded by others. The recollections remained dim, however, and unreal, not at all like those of a sober person

Of the 100 subjects studied, 36 reported having had complete blackouts, Goodwin's *en bloc* memory loss. The person has a sense of "lost time." All these 36 people could report precisely when the blackout began, but were less sure of when it ended. Most of Goodwin's subjects were aware of having blacked out only upon awakening from sleep. Twelve subjects, however, reported that they became aware of a blackout while awake. "One person found himself dancing with no recollection of what he had been doing during the previous six hours," Goodwin reported.

How long do the blackouts last? As Goodwin noted, it is difficult to determine because most end in sleep. Three men reported blackouts lasting longer than 48 hours. The longest lasted about five days.

How often did Goodwin's subjects have blackouts? First blackouts occurred in their mid-30s, on the average, and increased in both frequency and duration with age. Most of the subjects attributed this to increased drinking. Fourteen per cent of the people had experienced blackouts on one or two occasions. About a quarter of those experienced some degree of memory loss nearly every time they drank.

These 100 hospitalized alcoholics told Goodwin they behaved little differently during blackouts than they did during normal intoxication. The question is peculiar. How did they know?

The most disturbing characteristic of the blackouts, Goodwin said, involved travel. About a quarter of the subjects woke up in a place and had no memory of how they got there. Goodwin writes: "Often this involved traveling long distances over a period of a day or more. To negotiate such distances, the person obviously must have had certain control of his faculties. In some instances, checks had been written, planes boarded, hotels checked into, but the person could consciously recall none of these events."

Goodwin notes that subjects were told by friends, bartenders, bell captains and such, "You didn't seem very drunk. You had obviously been drinking, but behaved normally."

Goodwin adds: "Most subjects...had been told by observers that their behavior during the amnesic period had not been noticeably different from that of any person who had been drinking. If anything...they seemed less intoxicated during the blackout... than on other occasions."

Perhaps the most disturbing and frustrating characteristic of blackouts is their unpredictability, as Goodwin observed. Even confirmed alcoholics cannot anticipate when they will occur.

Consuming large quantities of alcohol will sometimes lead to a blackout and other times to a pass out. Even modest consumption can cause a blackout on occasion.

So, Goodwin talked to his subjects about the causes–he used the word "precipitants"–of their blackouts. Most believed that intoxication alone did not cause a blackout. All said they had been drunker and not blacked out. Asked to speculate about causes, the majority gave four possibilities: (1) drinking on an empty stomach or eating poorly in general; (2) being on a bender; (3) gulping drinks; (4) fatigue or not getting enough sleep.

Some other reasons given were drinking spirits instead of beer or wine; drinking shaving lotion or "canned heat;" psychological factors such as anxiety or depression. Goodwin said none of the blackout subjects reported "secondary gain," that is, they blacked out to escape the unpleasant consequences of their behavior.

Goodwin's study is valuable in understanding blackouts, but he unfortunately greatly confused the matter by including "fragmentary" memory loss in his discussion of blackouts. He was describing two different phenomena. Both may be brought on by alcohol, but result from different brain dysfunctions.

Goodwin described fragmentary amnesia as "off-and-on... memory loss where the person only realizes that he forgot an event when told about it later."

He described one man's experience this way: "A 53-year-old member of Alcoholics Anonymous said that he had experienced many 'blackouts' during his 25 years of heavy drinking. He could not remember his first blackout, but guessed it had happened about 15 years before. The memory loss had not bothered him, he said; he assumed everyone who drank had trouble with memory.

"Sometimes, however, it was 'embarrassing' to be told he had said something or gone somewhere and not recalled it. Upon being told, he would sometimes remember the event and sometimes not. Occasionally, months later, something would 'remind' him of the event and his memory would 'snap back.' Typically, he could remember some parts of a drinking episode and not others; a half hour might be blanked out and the next hour remembered. The forgotten parts appeared to have no more emotional significance than the remembered ones. 'It's like turning a switch on and off.'"

There is no doubt that fragmentary or on-and-off memory loss–I prefer the term fadeout to describe the experience–is a frequent occurrence during intoxication. An example is remembering answering the phone, but not who called or what was discussed. I have heard chronic or habitual drinkers report it as an almost daily occurrence. One of the terrors of the alcoholic is to wake up in the middle of the night and try to judge his degree of intoxication by what he can remember of the previous day, such as what he ate for dinner, who he talked to, where he went or what he did. Then he has to wait for daylight to begin the horrid task of quizzing relatives and friends (while appearing not to) in hopes of filling in the blanks.

But he does fill in the blanks, or many of them, which makes him entirely different (and much better off) than the blackout victim.

Studying fadeouts may be useful, but it has no relevance to blackouts. Goodwin was comparing apples and kiwis when he did. Again, the blackout victim never formed a memory. Obviously the fadeout victim did–only he's forgotten parts of it, not unexpected with heavy drinking.

Most importantly, the person in a fadeout was forming memory and cannot be considered unconscious.

In an effort to understand the fade out, it should be pointed out that the brain is selective in what it stores in memory, using little understood criteria to determine what should be stored in memory and what should be ignored or discarded. It seems obvious to me that the intoxicated person's fragmentary memory results from failure to pay attention or to attribute importance to words or events.

One of the most observed characteristics of the intoxicated person is his or her single mindedness. She fixates on a thought or idea, such as getting another drink, or perhaps on particular words or actions, repeating them over and over. Such fixation hardly contributes to awareness of what else is going on at the time. I suspect this person has not so much forgotten as she failed to see and hear or pay attention to what else was going on during the fixation.

Fadeouts may be a result of the chemical effects of alcohol on areas of the brain. It is worthy of serious study. But the mechanisms are different from those affected in the blackout. Nor is the fadeout a precursor of the blackout, as Goodwin thought.

The biggest problem with Goodwin's study is that he questioned only hospitalized alcoholics. To be hospitalized for alcoholism usually means the person has been a heavy drinker for a long time. Goodwin listed symptoms of alcoholism suffered by his subjects, such as liver disease, head trauma, fights, arrests, use of drugs, weekend drunks, morning drunks, benders, tremulousness, rum fits, DTs (delirium tremens), divorce, job loss and the ability to drink a fifth or more of whiskey per day.

If alcoholism is a continuum from 1 to 10, then these hospitalized drinkers were a 9. Their general health, their brains, including memory and judgment, have been so afflicted by long-term alcoholic consumption that even with detoxification and sobriety they will be years in approaching normal function.

Questioning such persons about blackouts may get answers, but more reliable ones might have come from a more general and representative population. Goodwin's subjects bear little resemblance to the Kevin Prices of this world in terms of background, education or life's experience.

I suspect Goodwin himself knew this. In another paper he mentions a study performed in 1946 for Alcoholics Anonymous. Thirty middle-aged social drinkers were interviewed. Nine or 30 per cent of them reported blackouts.

Then Goodwin adds: "In our own department (at Washington University in St. Louis), while interviewing young men for another study, it was found that nearly 40 per cent had experienced a blackout at least once. Their average age was 23. Many of these young men were light drinkers; typically, they had been drunk once or twice in their lifetimes, and on one or both of these occasions experienced memory loss. The men reporting blackouts by and large were lighter drinkers than those without such a history."

Goodwin says 40 per cent of these young, inexperienced drinkers had blackouts by age 23. In his study of hospitalized alcoholics only 8 per cent had known one at that age.

Goodwin goes on to suggest an interesting hypothesis. "The quantities of alcohol that alcoholics can consume is remarkable; even more remarkable is how little they seem physically affected by such heavy drinking, at least during the early years. Whether this tolerance for alcohol is innate or acquired is unknown, but it clearly exists. Perhaps as part of this general tolerance, even the memory of alcoholics is unusually resistant to alcohol. Conversely, just as proneness to nausea or vertigo from alcohol may keep many drinkers moderate, perhaps a proclivity for blackouts is part of a pattern of response to alcohol that discourages intemperance. Perhaps early blackouts predict not alcoholism but nonalcoholism."

As Goodwin says, it is a "hypothesis." What he really offers is tortured reasoning to justify his earlier statement declaring blackouts to be a symptom of alcoholism. "...our data suggest that the more severe the alcoholism the more likely blackouts are to occurs...and...only after years of heavy drinking and the alcoholism is well-established." If 30 per cent of social drinkers and 40 per cent of light drinkers experience blackouts, then ascribing them to alcoholism simply cannot be so. Had he interviewed a more general population, he might have discovered this.

Goodwin performed a second study in which he fed alcohol to volunteers in an effort to induce blackouts. As they became intoxicated, he planned to administer tests of their memory and intellectual functioning.

His study faced difficulties. To induce a blackout of the "nonrecovery" type, as he called it, very large amounts of alcohol must be consumed. But these amounts would be more than many social drinkers could consume without becoming ill or stuporous. Then they couldn't be tested.

To get around these problems Goodwin accepted 10 volunteers from among St. Louis day laborers looking for work. Again most were alcoholics. Five had a history of frequent blackouts. For his experiments, Goodwin provided between 16 and 18 ounces–a pint or more–of 86-proof bourbon whiskey. It was consumed at the rate of 6 oz. in the first hour and 4 oz per hour afterward. They were given tests to evaluate various types of memory and ability to perform calculation.

In these tests subjects were asked to recall a toy they were shown or to remember a brief scene from an erotic movie. These were tests of immediate and short-term memory. They were questioned about their childhood and about events that had occurred during the previous two days. These were tests of long-term or remote memory. Finally they were to perform some simple multiplication and subtraction problems.

So, what happened? Goodwin found that testing of all 10 subjects showed no impairment of long-term memory or ability to perform calculation. Five subjects had impairment of short-term memory. Toys and movie scenes recalled 30 minutes previously were no longer remembered. In four persons the short-term memory impairment began between the second and third hour of drinking. The fifth had memory loss toward the end of the fourth hour of drinking. None of the five did any better the next day. They had blacked out. All five, incidentally, were those who admitted to a history of blackouts before the test.

This is a valuable study. None of the five subjects who had blacked out were impaired in their ability to remember childhood events or perform math problems. This means their long-term memory was intact. They could remember what had occurred prior to blacking out.

When shown a toy for one minute, then asked two minutes later to name the toy (or describe the erotic movie scene) all remembered quite well. Thirty minutes later they had no memory of it at all. The blacked out persons had *immediate* memory but no *short-term* memory. A person in a blackout has memory of thoughts and ideas and what is going on for a short period of no more than a few minutes, then the memory disappears. In other words, the memory existed but was not stored. And, as Goodwin found out, the unstored memory can never be recovered.

Professor Goodwin was not the only one to study blackouts during this period. A group of doctors* employed by the National Center for Prevention and Control of Alcoholism, part of the National Institute of Mental Health in Chevy Chase, MD. performed a well-conceived study.

*They were John S. Tamerin, M.D., Sheldon Weiner, M. D., Roger Poppen, PH.D., Peter Steinglass, M.D., Jack H. Mendelson, M.D.

These doctors noted that some clinicians deny any real impairment of memory occurs and view blackouts as malingering. All events are recalled, but are consciously withheld to avoid responsibility or punishment. Is this true?

To find out, the experimenters selected 13 male alcoholic volunteers between the ages of 26 and 39, all with histories of repeated blackouts, but no memory defects when sober. All were brought into a hospital in the Washington, D.C., area and kept sober for 10 days while they were tested. Then came a free-choice drinking period of 12 to 14 days during which the subjects could obtain up to a quart of 100-proof alcohol each day.

Their blood alcohol levels were tested by Breathalyzer three times a day. Their short-term memories were tested at one, five and 30-minute intervals using standard picture and box tests. They were questioned at 24-hour intervals about events of the previous day. All the subjects were heavy smokers, but the only way they could get a cigarette was by giving correct answers to tests. The experimenters felt this would discourage malingering.

Results were tabulated and graphed for sober, moderate and heavy drinking. The trend was definitely downward. The more alcohol consumed, the worse the recall. The memory that had been near 100 per cent when sober fell drastically to less than half or one-third in some cases and all the way to zero in a few.

So much for malingering.

In this study as well as earlier ones by Goodwin, the researchers were led down a blind alley, in my opinion, when they investigated something called "state-dependent memory." The idea is that a blacked out drinker may forget something sober, but he will remember it when he's again drunk.

Goodwin asked his 100 hospitalized alcoholics if they had "ever hidden money or alcohol while drinking, forgotten it while sober, and had their memory return during later drinking." Sixty-one percent said they had. Before being asked, 12 said drink seemed to improve their recall and 10 said they sometimes drank for that express purpose.

Goodwin: "A 47-year-old housewife often wrote letters when she was drinking. Sometimes she would jot down notes for a letter and start writing it, but not finish it. The next day, sober, she would be unable to decipher the notes. Then she would start drinking again, and after a few drinks the meaning of the notes would become clear and she would resume writing the letter. 'It was like picking up the pencil where I had left off.'"

Goodwin designed experiments hoping to discover whether state-dependent memory existed. Could a few drinks return memory to a blackout victim?

One of the attractions of alcohol, a reason people drink it at all, is to produce the well-known "high," in which inhibitions fall away and the person becomes more alert and stimulated. It doesn't last long. Depression inevitably follows. So the person keeps on drinking in an effort to keep the high or to recover it.

I suspect state-dependent memory is mostly the alcohol-produced high. It may help that woman decipher her scribbled notes, but it will do absolutely nothing to help the Kevin Price's of this world remember what happened during a blackout, as Dr. Goodwin himself discovered.

Despite flaws, the work of Goodwin and the others was promising. It confirmed that blackouts do occur among alcoholics and that blackouts can be induced among alcoholics. Some of the characteristics of blackouts were described.

Then the work ended. Goodwin reported blackouts among moderate and light drinkers, yet he never followed up on it. A later study in San Diego proved that light drinkers could have blackouts if much alcohol was consumed, but again that was not followed up.

No work was done to pursue the causes of the blackouts. How does alcohol interfere with memory? It was a question begging an answer. Goodwin had an inkling, writing "the hippocampus may ultimately be shown to play a role in the memory disturbance." Then he did nothing about it.

One must ask why.

16

Falling Through The Cracks

The study of blackouts begun so promisingly in the early 1970s was largely abandoned, leaving a void in our knowledge that has continued to this day.

Ethical difficulties may have forced an end. Giving large quantities of alcohol to subjects, whether paid or volunteer, to try to induce blackouts was not to be encouraged on medical or ethical grounds. Addiction, perhaps serious injury could result. The gain in knowledge was considered not worth that risk. We already know alcohol can cause blackouts, so don't drink. Next problem please.

We need to consider this ethical matter. As already pointed out, Goodwin seriously erred in testing hospitalized alcoholics. He assumed, along with most other people, that blackouts were a symptom of advanced alcoholism, along with DTs, shakes, rum fits and all the rest. Only belatedly did he come to realize light and moderate drinkers also black out.

In my opinion, no research justifies giving alcohol in any amounts, large or small, to alcoholics. Their very lives are being put at risk. But young, nonalcoholic volunteers might be permissible. For example, a group of college students, perhaps with experience in blackouts from binge drinking, might be collected and tested under controlled conditions. If they were photographed, their behavior might induce them to control their consumption. Such persons would certainly provide far more useful information on blackouts than hospitalized alcoholics.

Another possibility exists. The science of anesthesiology may offer a way to study blackouts.

Anesthetizing a patient for surgery involves several steps. (See Fig. 6) First, the patient must lose the ability to remember anything that happens during surgery. Despite the best efforts of anesthetists, patients do sometimes remember conversations and other events in the OR. This is a major concern to anesthetists, whose journal *Anesthesiology*, regularly publishes articles on the occurrence of learning and memory during general anesthesia.

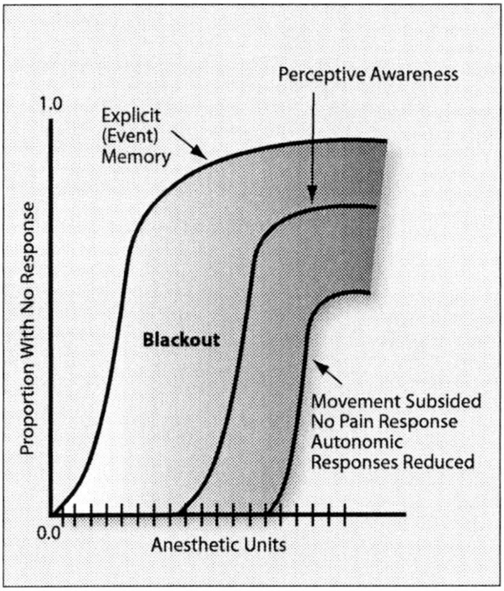

Fig. 6 Range of Alcohol Blackout

As the dose of anaesthesia increases, he next loses perceptive awareness, that is, knowledge of what is going on around him and is happening to him in the OR. In the third stage of "going under," the patient loses the ability to feel pain. Fourth, he loses the ability to move. After all he must remain still during surgery. Finally, with enough anaethetic, the patient loses control of his involuntary actions (autonomic system), such as breathing.

My reading would indicate if it is possible, using some of the newer anesthetics, to induce amnesia yet leave the patient conscious? Said another way, would it be possible to give a person just enough anesthetic to halt memory formation, yet leave him conscious with normal perceptive awareness and other functions? If so, then a person similar to Henry M. or the blacked out individual might be created. She could be studied without fear of addiction or other harmful effects of excessive alcohol consumption.

To my knowledge, no anesthetist has attempted to create such a state. Yet it seems to me it might be possible. Many modern anesthetics are variations of ether and thus alcohol. The anesthetics achieve their results by affecting the brain much in the same manner as alcohol, that is, by inhibiting either the NMDA or GABA mechanisms.

Certain it is, if blackouts can be induced by anesthetics, then a whole new avenue of study might be opened.

Returning to Goodwin, I think something else may have led him to abandon his research almost as soon as it started. He was a psychiatrist in a school of medicine, and pursuit of the causes of blackouts would lead him out of his chosen field. He perhaps left it for neuroscientists to continue his work.

I suspect study of blackouts fell through the cracks of science. Neuroscientists were probing the brain, learning exciting stuff about how memory works, frequently using rats, monkeys and other animals. They were not particularly interested in psychology, alcoholism, medicine and other fields of study involved in blackouts. Psychiatrists couldn't solve the problem without getting into neuroscience–not their field.

And so it remained. Psychiatry texts, if they mentioned blackouts at all, cited Goodwin's work as definitive. Cause? Too much alcohol. Treatment? Drink less alcohol.

Readers who have remained with me this far have encountered quotations or references to work from psychologists, neurologists and neuroscientists, as well as psychiatrists. Perhaps we ought to review just who these people are.

According to the Merriam-Webster College Dictionary, Tenth Edition, psychiatry is "a branch of medicine that deals with mental, emotional or behavioral disorders;" *psychology* is "the science of mind and behavior."; neurology is the "scientific study of the nervous system esp. (especially) in respect to its structure, function and abnormalities:" and *neuroscience* is "a branch of the life sciences that deals with the anatomy, physiology, biochemistry, or molecular biology of nerves and nervous tissue and esp. with their relation to behavior and learning."

Some interesting distinctions there. And there is certainly plenty of room for all four of these specialties to contribute to our knowledge of the brain. And all are contributing. The problem is they rarely get together to discover it. Scientists in each field report their discoveries in separate medical and scientific journals, each with its own terminology and methodology. But none of it is applied to the problem of the alcohol blackout. An interdisciplinary approach is needed.

Okay, fine. But why did this neglect of blackouts continue so long, even into a new millennium?

Perhaps it was all those jokes about drunks too besotted to find their way home. So, he doesn't remember anything the next day. What of it? Serves him right for overindulging. Mostly he's going to sober up and recover. So he doesn't remember a few hours. Who cares? And, if he did something wrong, there was always the law to throw away the key.

The argument may be made that the blackout is a little like the common cold or the canker sore. Both are unpleasant for a while, but the victim recovers on her own. Study and research to find out causes and prevention is hardly worth the investment. There are several serious, usually congenital diseases that remain neglected because the incidence of the disease is too small to justify the expenditure.

And so our disinterest in blackouts continued. If someone, on the Internet, say, inquired about blackouts, Goodwin's research was cited. He'd worked with hospitalized alcoholics, so blackouts remained a problem of heavy drinking and advanced alcoholism. That blackouts might occur among light and moderate drinkers remained a curiosity, a speculation. Binge drinking was viewed as a lark, kids being kids. Warnings about the possibly harmful effects of blackouts were seldom heard.

Henry M. became a subject of intense study to psychologists and neuroscientists. Here was a man unable to form memory. A huge curiosity, he was studied and tested, and a great deal was learned about the role of memory in daily life. But, in truth, much of the testing of Henry was foolish investigation into the content of his dreams and what inkblots looked like to him. No one considered that he was in an unconscious state much like a person in a blackout. A perhaps unique opportunity to study the role of memory in human consciousness was lost.

Much as Goodwin had predicted, the role of the hippocampus in memory formation was probed. Even when the role of alcohol in blocking NMDA receptors and memory formation was discovered, it hardly made a ripple. True, the literature began to reflect this new knowledge, but not its ramifications.

As we saw in the Cox case, an expert witness on blackouts knew that "neurological, chemical processes by which we form permanent memory stops operating." He then got the effects of this exactly backwards, saying the person still has short-term memory but cannot remember something learned years before.

It follows as night unto day that if NMDA *receptors are blocked by alcohol then (1) the person is forming no memory and (2) if he forms no memory he is unconscious, even though he is walking, talking and awake.*

At this writing I have not yet found in the literature where anyone is reporting these two central facts. And I do not understand why it is not being reported.

There is something else I don't understand. When Goodwin gave alcohol to his subjects, five of them blacked out. He knew this because he tested them. Something remembered for two minutes was not recalled a half hour later or the next day. Goodwin discovered that they could remember long ago events and do arithmetic calculations. And that's about all he reported.

Think about it a moment. Here was Goodwin, professor of psychiatry at a major medical school, alone in his lab with five blacked out men. He had succeeded in creating five men–not one but five Henry M.'s–who were unable to form memory.

Lord, what an opportunity! They could be observed, questioned and tested. The parameters of consciousness could be limned. At the very least they could be tape recorded and photographed–all easily available in 1970–so later researchers could make use of their condition.

Goodwin made an immense discovery. He found that in the alcohol blackout the person keeps his immediate memory, his long-term memory and his procedural memory, but loses his working memory, as it was later called. This is of staggering importance.

Goodwin was content not to go further with it. Okay, fine, but one would think, wouldn't one, that other researchers would have picked up on this and probed the unanswered questions?

- Precisely how long does the immediate memory last? Seconds, minutes? Does he lose the immediate memory if distracted? When the immediate memory fades, what replaces it?
- What are the effects of loss of short-term memory on talk and actions? What can this person do and not do? If left alone, how does he act?
- Is he capable of thought? Can he solve a problem, learn information, make a decision, carry it out? Is he in fact conscious?

The questions go on and on. A huge portal for research was opened. Hundred of studies were possible. Thousands of papers could be written. Man's knowledge of his mind, memory and consciousness could have been forever expanded.

A few tentative steps were taken into the unknown beyond the portal. Then it was slammed shut, never to be opened again.

I don't understand it. Are we dealing with monumental lack of curiosity? Or something else? I don't pretend to even begin to understand the whole political and economic process of obtaining money, equipment and authority for research projects. That's another study entirely.

But I strongly suspect that whatever the process is it allows deserving areas of study to fall through the cracks, remaining misunderstood and ignored. And I have an idea this sort of thing happens rather frequently.

While I'm stepping on the toes of colleagues, I might as well offer another theory to explain how blackouts fell through the cracks of medicine. Fortunately for me, I am not alone in faulting psychiatry for (1) its decades-long enamorment with the now discredited Freudian theory, and (2) its insistence on studying the mind rather than the brain.

Intellect, thought and emotions, all produced by the mind,

are brain functions. The mind may be said to be a product of the brain. And the brain is where exciting scientific work is occurring.

Neuroscientists discovered the effect of alcohol on NMDA receptors, enabling even a doctor of internal medicine to understand what a blackout is. At the same time many psychiatrists continue to insist the blackout is dissociative behavior, perhaps Freudian repression, even malingering.

My point is that psychiatry, because of its absorption with Freudian theory and the mind-vs.-brain, failed to understand blackouts and neglected a chance to probe the nature of consciousness. In so doing, psychiatry is at risk of becoming less than mainstream science, even redundant.

If psychiatry is going to lay claim to alcoholism and addiction as its medical specialty, then it should study and perform research. Virtually ignoring the blackout in its DSM-IV isn't at all helpful. It smacks of mirrors and snake oil.

I used the medical model of the common cold or canker sore to explain the lack of study of blackouts. But I can think of other medical models that hopefully will apply.

For decades, at least, common or three-day measles was considered a minor blip in childhood, the least of all childhood diseases. Then it was discovered that measles had serious repercussions for health. A vaccine was soon developed.

After decades of treating ulcers with antacids and bland diets, it was discovered that at least some ulcers are a result of a bacteria and antibiotics are effective treatment.

More recently, Rohypnol and the other date rape drugs were found to cause blackouts (see appendix). The peril to young women was realized and a national educational campaign launched to warn them.

I hope for something similar, new awareness of the dangers of blackouts, particularly to young people, and a campaign to alert them to the dangers. But we also need study and research, a great deal of it. This we consider next.

17
An Open Door

I suggested that when Donald Goodwin and his colleagues studied blackouts 30-plus years ago, they opened a wide portal for study–a door that promptly closed. In the last chapter I described some possible reasons for the closure. Now I want to envision what might lie ahead if the door is reopened.

The basic mystery of the blackout has been solved. We now know that alcohol blocks NMDA receptors and perhaps more in the brain, preventing memory formation until the effects of the alcohol wears off. Knowing that no memory is being formed allows simple memory tests to be administered to recognize when a person is in a blackout.

These are huge discoveries. The door to research is now opened. All we have to do is walk through it.

Hopefully it is already being done, but scientists now need to hook up blacked out persons to EEG, MRI and PET scan equipment so they can compare their brain activity to a sober, non-blacked out person. If the brain activity of the person in a blackout is also compared to those asleep or in a coma or under anesthetics, we could increase our understanding of consciousness. Certainly we would discover the limitations of the blacked out person.

But the door is not just open to scientists using expensive apparatus. Obviously Goodwin's studies need to be resumed and expanded. Controlled studies and testing should reveal the precise nature of the blackout; what types of memory are not being formed; whether immediate, long-term and procedural memories are entirely intact or partially damaged; what the parameters are of ability to learn, form intent, reach and carry out decisions; how senses are affected; what stimulants bring what reactions; reactions to stress; the effect of emotions on behavior; changes in personality during the blackout; tendencies toward violence....

And much more. Endlessly more.

So wide is this portal that graduate and even undergraduate students can enter, performing original work and publishing the results. We desperately need to know, and with as much accuracy as possible, what type of drinking precipitates the blackout. I have suggested drinking rapidly on an empty stomach while fatigued may induce the blackout. But this could be wrong, wholly or in part. There may be other contributing factors.

No MRI machine is needed. Just stay sober at a frat or dorm party. Simply observe who drinks what how fast and who acts spacey and "out of it." A casual test of short-term memory should reveal the person in a blackout. He can then be questioned and observed in a careful manner. Even better, perhaps he can be recorded or video taped for later analysis.

Such studies could be invaluable, especially if organized and supervised by faculty. Chances are only in this way will we solve the riddle of why drinking causes a blackout one time but not the next. Solution to this riddle may lead to prevention of the blackout entirely.

The studies of blacked out persons may help us understand their attitudes and actions, their limitations and tendencies. We may learn how to handle them, get them home safely, and keep them from harming themselves and others.

Law enforcement and jurisprudence ought to eagerly await studies of the blacked out person, his abilities and limitations, what can be expected from him and how he might be controlled.

And, I cannot help believing that in probing blackouts we may move closer to understanding consciousness and thereby our very humanity.

Finally, I am also willing to believe that study of blackouts may produce information and insights not yet dreamed of.

Whatever happens, it is past time we take the alcohol blackout seriously, abandon the jokes, decry our collective ignorance, and set out to discover exactly what happens when a human being is unconscious while awake and seemingly functional.

That it happens at all, let alone so often, and we can neither understand nor prevent it, is only remarkable. It is not just past time we studied blackouts, it is way, way, way past time.

End

Appendix
Other Blackout Drugs

Suicide was about the last thing anyone expected from Morton Ungar. Everyone knew the 53-year-old as a loving husband and father, good friend, responsible provider. He had no emotional problems anyone knew of. And his health was pretty good. He had a little prostate trouble, but his doctor was treating that. He also gave Ungar a prescription for Halcion to help him sleep better.

Shortly thereafter Ungar suddenly began to change, becoming more agitated, quiet, less sociable. His family and friends noticed it. Still it came as a total shock, when, a month later, without warning, Ungar threw himself off the top of a hotel.

Ungar's wife Doris sued The Upjohn Company, maker of Halcion, and the physician. Without admitting any of the charges, Upjohn settled the case before trial. The doctor's malpractice trial resulted in a $1.2 million award to Mrs. Unger.

In another case, sheriff's deputies from Hurricane, Utah, found 83-year-old Mildred Coats lying on her bed, a happy birthday card clutched in her left hand, eight bullet wounds in her head. The woman's daughter, Ilo Grundberg, 57, handed deputies a written confession, "I didn't kill her because I didn't love her. I loved her very much."

Ms. Grundberg was arrested, charged with second-degree murder, then moved to a mental hospital in Salt Lake City for examination. Psychiatrists declared she was involuntarily intoxicated from the drug Halcion when she murdered her mother. She had no motive for the murder and little memory of it. Prosecutors dropped the charges. Ilo Grundberg went free.

Ms. Grundberg promptly sued The Upjohn Company, calling the drug "defective," and demanding $21 million in penalties because Upjohn failed to notify the public of the "severe and sometimes fatal adverse reactions" to the medicine. Upjohn insisted it was "in no way negligent," then announced it had settled the case out of court, the details of which were to remain confidential.

These cases are sad. When Halcion came on the market in the early 1970s, it qualified as a wonder drug, at least among sleeping potions. If a person took Halcion, she fell asleep quickly and woke up bright and alert the next morning. Previous sleeping pills, notably the barbituates, left the person groggy and hung over the morning after.

At its peak in the early 1990s, Halcion was sold in more than 90 countries under various names. It was Upjohn's second biggest money-maker (after the closely related tranquilizer Xanax). In the U. S. alone, a half million prescriptions for Halcion were filled every month.

Then the troubles started. Reports of amnesia, anxiety, delusions, hostility began to surface. Cases like Morton Ungar and Mildred Coats made headlines. Newsweek and Time did cover articles on Halcion. Journalists couldn't resist the headline, "The Dark Side of Halcion."

Britain and the Netherlands banned the drug. There were repeated calls in the U. S. for the FDA (Food and Drug Administration) to do the same. The FDA ordered repeated tests, concluding after each series that Halcion was safe if used as directed. It seems that triazolam, the active drug in Halcion, was to be used occasionally when sleep eluded a person. It was never intended for long-term use, no more than a week or 10 days consecutively. The problems resulted from long-term use of the sleeping pill.

Nonetheless, Upjohn (now known as Pharmacia) reduced the strength of Halcion from l mg of triazolam to 0.25 mg. If taken as directed the drug is considered safe. Certain it is that people with sleep disorders find it useful.

So, what's the story of Halcion doing in a book on alcohol blackouts? The reader may have already noted that "amnesia" was listed among the adverse side effects of the drug. Psychiatrists examining Ilo Grundberg said she had little memory of killing her mother. Forgetfulness became a frequent complaint of long-term Halcion takers.

One of the uses for Halcion is on long air flights. Pop a pill, go to sleep, wake up at your destination, refreshed and ready to go. I have trouble going to sleep on airplanes and have found Halcion helpful in dozing off, but I've taken only the quarter mg. dose.

When the strength was l mg., Upjohn received complaints of "traveler's amnesia," as it was called. People were not just falling asleep on flights, they couldn't remember going to the airport, eating, landing and picking up their luggage. This is scary, of course. What else isn't remembered?

This sounds a lot like the imbiber waking up from an alcohol blackout, doesn't it?

But there are important differences. There are no other signs of drunkenness associated with Halcion. The user does not stagger, lisp, act the fool—unless these are normal conditions for him. He simply does not remember certain things that he should.

And something else happens which makes the Halcion blackout different from the alcoholic. The Halcion blackout is often *retrograde*. The user forgets events before he took the pill, such as driving to the airport, checking in, getting on the plane.

The alcohol blackout, on the other hand, is never retrograde.

There are a lot of questions to ask about the role of Halcion in memory, but first we must consider another, closely related, even more famous drug, Rohypnol, the so-called "date rape" drug. Both belong to a family of drugs called benzodiazepines. These include Valium, Librium, Ativan, Serax, Klonopin and Dalmane, among others. All affect memory, especially when consumed with alcohol.

Rohypnol is banned in the U. S. because of its nefarious and illegal use. Actually it is a useful drug. Made by the Hoffman-La Roche Company, it is prescribed as a short-term treatment for severe insomnia, and as a sedative hypnotic and a preanesthetic. Rohypnol has physiological effects similar to Valium (diazepam), but it is approximately ten times more potent.

Rohypnol is highly addictive. Memorable scenes in the Oscar-nominated film, "Ulee's Gold," portrayed Ulee's daughter-in-law suffering violent drug withdrawal. The drug she supposedly used was Rohypnol.

Who first discovered Rohypnol could be used to render women helpless to rape is unknown–at least to me. Also unknown to me is who would want to and what sort of appeal such an attack might have for the perpetrator. The woman is unconscious, unaware of what the man is doing to her, unlikely to remember it afterwards. How this becomes in any way superior to masturbation escapes me. But then there is no accounting for juvenile propensities among the criminally inclined. That the drug has found its greatest use on college campuses suggests that admission standards need to be upgraded.

In the movie *High Society* based on the play and movie *The Philadelphia Story*, a love-struck and sauced Frank Sinatra carries a tipsy Grace Kelly up to her room, puts her to bed and leaves, later explaining, "There are rules about such things." Obviously, the rules are unknown to dispensers of date rape drugs.

Imported from abroad, often Mexico, the drug comes in presealed bubble packs of one or two mg doses. The tablets are white, bearing the word "ROCHE" on one side. This led to the nickname "roches, roofies, roopies, ruffies." It is also called "the forget pill," "mind-erasers," and "trip-and-fall." It is cheap, costing about $5 a pill.

Rohypnol is soluble to water, beer, liquor or other liquids. When dissolved it is largely odorless and tasteless. It takes effect within minutes, with the victim experiencing drowsiness, light-headedness, dizziness, fatigue, memory loss, slurred speech, loss of motor coordination, impaired judgment, severe loss of inhibition and coma–more or less in that order, depending on how much of the drug was ingested. The effects peak within two hours and can persist for up to eight hours.

Victims ingesting Rohypnol along with alcohol in sufficient quantities have had blackouts lasting as long as 24 hours.

The drug normally disappears from the system in 48 hours.

All these properties make the drug highly appealing to rapists. It is easily slipped into a girl's beverage at a bar, club or party. She quickly becomes disoriented, then helpless. If she has any memories of the entire encounter, they will be fleeting. If she remembers even being raped, chances are that she will be unable to identify her attacker–or prove an attack occurred.

Use of Rohypnol has lessened, largely because of an extensive nationwide campaign to alert young women to the risks of accepting opened drinks or leaving their glasses unattended. Hoffman-LaRoche has aided these efforts by altering the drug so that a liquid turns blue when Rohypnol is dropped into it.

Unfortunately other, similar drugs have come along, notably

Ketamine, Clonazepam, Scopalamine. By far the worst, closely mimicking Rohypnol, is GHB (gamma-hydroxybutrate). Its street names include "liquid ecstasy," "soma-tomax," "scoop," and "grievous bodily harm." The latter name is most apt.

All the date-rape drugs create blackouts similar to those brought on by alcohol. Along with loss of motor control, judgment and inhibition, these drugs cause memory loss. It has to be a truly terrifying experience for a young woman to suspect she might have been raped and then have no memory of it or whom she was with. No wonder the drugs are outlawed.

But there are some signal differences. The date rape drugs are also retrograde. A period of time before the drug was consumed is blacked out. The victim may not remember being in the bar or whom she was with.

Again, retrograde memory loss never occurs with the alcohol blackout.

In it the alcohol blocks the NMDA receptors in the hippocampus, stopping formation of short-term memory. Halcion, Rohypnol and the other benzodiazepines cause memory losses that are similar, yet significantly different. Halcion produces no symptoms of inebriation, while Rohypnol does. Both create retrograde memory loss, while alcohol does not.

Clearly some other or additional brain mechanism is at work. I know of no research to even try to discover this alternative pathway to a blackout. I can only guess that it involves perhaps another neurotransmitter such as GABA. The pathway may not even go through the hippocampus at all.

In preparing this chapter, I contacted Pharmacia, formerly Upjohn, to ask if they had any unpublished studies of Halcion that might be useful to me. They were kind enough to send me a half-inch thick sheath of reports.

Nowhere in these or in published reports have I found any indication that Pharmacia-Upjohn attempted to discover how or why its drug Halcion caused blackouts. How unfortunate! Think of the opportunity to enhance human knowledge. By exploring and exposing how Halcion causes memory loss and blackouts, Upjohn might have begun to understand how consciousness occurs in the human brain.

Pharmacia-Upjohn did not pursue such inquiries, nor did the FDA require it. Pharmacia simply cut the dose of triazolan from 1 mg to .25 mg, so the period of unconsciousness no longer occurred. The FDA was satisfied with that.

I know I am at risk of beating a dead horse, but how is it possible in a supposedly enlightened and scientific nation to allow blackouts to occur without understanding the process by which they happen. We are at risk of knowing more about pulsars, quasars and black holes than we do about what happens inside our skulls.

Another incongruity comes to mind. Both Halcion and Rohypnol have achieved what might be called "star status" in the U. S. Both made magazine covers. Rohypnol and the other date rape drugs made the rounds of talk shows. The FDA brought to bear its regulatory powers. Rohypnol was made illegal in this country. Laws were written to punish those using drugs to rape women. Rape crisis centers were alerted to help victims. A massive campaign to educate young women about the illegal use of Rohypnol was funded and mounted.

I have no quarrel with any of this. The situation demanded action and we took action. Simply wonderful.

But there is another drug, far cheaper and easier to obtain, and legally so, which causes perhaps millions of blackouts every day. Yet alcohol has none of the attributes of "star status." Is it because alcohol is not associated with nubile, college girls, but with drunken sots curled up in skidrow doorways?

Reduce it to a more human level. Kevin Price went to a party and began to drink beer. He had no idea that a blackout could occur in which he walked, talked, appeared conscious but wasn't. He had never heard of such a thing. In his blackout state he drives off, kills five people, and goes to prison.

There are educational campaigns reporting the evils of drink, but no specific warnings about the risks of blackouts, no lists of warning signs, no tips for prevention.

Loss of memory, blackouts and unconscious states are side effects of alcohol. Users are at risk every time they swallow the substance, just as users of Halcion and Rohypnol are. Perhaps it's time to afford equal treatment for alcohol, both in terms of research and prevention.

Sources

There is a huge and rapidly growing literature, perhaps millions of articles and books, dealing with the human brain, memory and consciousness. Yet the literature on the alcohol blackout is minuscule and mostly stagnant—certainly a measure of our societal problem.

This list only hints at the knowledge that is out there. What I have tried to do in this list is provide the sources for material quoted or cited in the text and to offer some assistance to readers seeking more information.

Books

Baars, Bernard J., Ed.; *Essential Sources in the Scientific Study of Consciousness;* Massachusetts Institute of Technology, Boston, 2003.

Baddeley, Alan D.; *The Psychology of Memory;* Basic Books, Inc., New York, 1976.

Bloom, Floyd F.; *Brain, Mind and Behavior;* Educational Broadcasting Corp., 1985.

Carey, Joseph, Ed.; *Brain Facts;* The Society or Neuroscience, Washington, D.C., 2002.

"Chuck C."; *A new Pair of Glasses;* New Look Publishing Co., Irvine, CA, 1984.

Crick, Francis; *The Astonishin Hypothesis: The Scientific Search for the Soul;* Simon & Shuster, New York, 1994.

Churchland, Paria Smith; *Brain-Wise: Studies in Neurophilosophy;* Massachusetts Institute of Technology, Boston, 2002.

Damasio, Antonio R.; *Descartes' Error: Emotion, Reason and the Human Brain;* G. P. Putnam's Sons, New York, 1994.

Edelman, Gerald M., M.D.; *Wider Than the Sky: The Phenomenal Gift of Consciousness,* Yale University Press, New Haven, CT. 2004.

Eichenbaum, Howard; *The Cognitive Neuroscience of Memory: An Introduction;* Oxford University Press, New York, 2002.

Eichenbaum, Howard and Cohen, Neal J.; *From Conditioning to Conscious Recollection: Memory Systems of the Brain;* Oxford University Press, New York, 200l.

Goodman, Louis Sanford and Gilman, Alfred; *The Pharmacological Basis of Therapeutics;* The McGraw-Hill Companies, New York, 2001.

Hilts, Philip J.; *Memory's Ghost: The Nature of Memory and the Strange Tale of Mr. M.;* Simon & Shuster, New York,1995.

Huber, Peter; *Galileo's Revenge: Junk Science in the Courtroom;* Basic Books, New York, 1991.

Kapur, Narinder; *Memory Disorders in Clinical Practice;* Butterworth & Co.,London, 1988.

LeDoux, Joseph; *Synaptic Self: How our Brains Become Who We Are;* Viking, New York, 2002.

Pinker, Steven; *The Blank Slate; The Modern Denial of Human Nature;* Viking, New York, 2002.

Rhodes, Richard; *Why They Kill;* Alfred A. Knopf, New York, 1999.

Schacter, Daniel L.; *Searching for Memory: The Brain, the Mind and the Past;* Basic Books, New York, 1996.

Simon, Robert I., Ed.; *Review of Clinical Psychiatry and the Law;* American Psychiatric Press, Washington, D..C. 1992

Squire, Larry R.; *Mind Matters: How Mind and Brain Interact to Create our Conscious Lives;* Oxford University Press, New York, 1987.

Terr, Lenore; *Unchained Memories;* Basic Books, New York, 1994.

Vaillant, George E.; *The Natural History of Alcoholism Revisited;* Harvard University Press; 2000.

Wholey, Dennis; *The Courage to Change;* Delacorte Press, New

York, 1984.

Zeman, Adam; *Consciousness: A User's Guide;* Yale University Press, New Haven, CT, 2002.

Articles

Bolan, Barbara, etal; "A Comparison of Three Tests to Detect Feigned Amnesia: The Effects of Feedback and the Measurement of Response Latency"; *Journal of Clinical and Experimental Neuropsychology,* 2002, Vol. 24, No. 2.

Campagna, Jason A., etal; "Mechanisms of Actions of Inhaled Anesthetics"; *New England Journal of Medicine,* May 22, 2003.

Charness, Michael E., etal; "Ethanol and the Nervous System"; *The New England Journal of Medicine,* August 17, 1989.

Cima, M., etal; "I Can't Remember Your Honor: Offenders Who Claim Amnesia"; *German Journal of Psychiatry,* 2001.

Corkin, Suzanne; "What's New with the Amnesic Patient H.M.?"; *Neroscience,* February, 2002.

Dichenbaum, Howard; "The Long and Winding Road to Memory Consolidation"; *Neuroscience,* November 2001.

Goodwin, Donald W.; "The Muse and the Martini"; JAMA, April 2, 1973.

"Two Species of Alcholic 'Blackout'"; *American Journal of Psychiatry,* June, 1971.

"Phenomenological Aspects of the Alcoholic 'Blackout' "; *British Journal of Psychiatry,* p. 1033, 1969.

"Blackouts and Alcohol-Induced Memory Dysfunction"; *Mello and Mendelson, Recent Advances in Studies of Alcoholism,* p. 508, 1971.

"Alcoholic 'Blackouts' Review and Clinical Study of 100 Alcoholics"; *American Journal of Psychiatry,* p. 19, 1969.

"Loss of Short-Term Memory as a Predictor of the Alcoholic 'Blackout' "; *Nature,* p. 227: 201, 1970.

"Alcohol and Recall: State-Dependent Effects in Man"; *Science,* 163:1358, 1969.

Jellinek, E. M.; "Phases in the Drinking History of Alcoholics"; *Quarterly Journal of Studies of Alcoholism;* 7:1-88, 1946.

Kandel, Eric R. and Squire, Larry R.; "Neuroscience: Breaking Down Scientific Barriers to the Study of Brain and Mind"; *Science,* November 10, 2000.

Loftus, Elizabeth; "Our Changeable Memories: Legal and Practical Implications"; *Neuroscience,* March, 2003.

Ghoneim, M. M. and Block, Robert I; "Learning and Memory During General Anesthesia"; *Anesthesiology,* August 1997.

Oscar-Berman, Marlene, etal; "Impairments of Brain and Behavior; The Neurological Effects of Alcohol"; *Alcohol, Health & Research World,* Vol. 21, 1997.

Ryback, Ralph S.; "The Continuum and Specificity of the Effects of Alcohol on Memory"; *Quarterly Journal of the Studies of Alcoholism*, p. 995, 1971.

Squire, Larry R.; "Mechanisms of Memory"; *Science*, June, 1986.

Sweeney, Donal F.; "Impaired Physician"; *Medical Economics*, 1982.

"Questions You Always Wanted to Ask About AA"; *Postgraduate Medicine*.

"Alcohol & Mnemosyne: Blackouts"; *Journal of Substance Abuse Treatment*, September, l989.

"Blackouts Legal Implications"; *Journal of Substance Abuse Treatment*, September 1990.

Tamerin, John S., etal; "Alcohol and Memory: Amnesia and Short-term Memory Function During Experimentally Induced Intoxication"; *American Journal of Psychiatry*, June 1971.

Wickelgren, Ingrid; "Getting a Grasp on Working Memory"; *Science Magazine*, July 5, 2000.

Tsai, Guochuan, etal; "The Glutamatergic Basis of Human Alcoholism"; *American Journal of Psychiatry*, March, 1995.

White, Aaron M.; "Alcohol-Induced Blackouts"; *copyrighted and published on the Internet*, January, 2.

About The Authors

DONAL F. SWEENEY, M.D. is board certified in internal medicine, chest disease and addiction medicine. He is a Fellow of the American Society of Addiction Medicine. Dr. Sweeney served as a doctor with the Air Force from 1962-91, rising to the rank of Colonel, then maintained a private practice in Santa Barbara, California. In 1990 he was named Director of Occupational Health Services and Employee Assistance at the Jet Propulsion Laboratory in Pasadena, California. He semi-retired in 2000. Dr. Sweeney is author of numerous articles on alcoholism and blackouts. In 2002 the Jet Propulsion Laboratory honored him by naming a six-kilometer asteroid after him. He lives in Santa Barbara with his wife Jo.

Dr. Sweeney describes his personal quest which led to this book. It began in the mid-1980s during a lecture on alcoholism at the University of California, Santa Barbara, when a student asked, "What's a blackout?"

Dr. Sweeney realized he didn't know the answer. The more he studied, the more he discovered how little was known about blackouts. He was led far afield from his specialty in internal medicine. Indeed, the answers he sought depended on neurostudies just being performed and reported.

There is still much to be learned, but Dr. Sweeney now answers the question, revealing the blackout to be a neglected, often devastating condition that has fallen through the cracks of medicine and the law.

Robert A. Liston, a former newspaperman and magazine journalist, is the author of 50 nonfiction books. Among these is *The Waysiders: A New Approach to Reading and the Dyslexic Child,* written with R.M.N. Crosby, M.D. It was the first book to call attention to dyslexia as a reading disorder. It was published twice in the US and in the UK. Reviewers lauded it for discussing a complex subject in lucid terms. Some called it a new approach to scientific writing.

Liston also collaborated on *The Pill: Facts and Fallacies About Today's Contraceptives* by Robert W. Kistner, M.D. The intricacies of female endocrine and reproductive systems were explained in easily understood terms.

Liston is the sole author of two books on psychology, *When Reason Fails* and *Healing the Mind.* Among his 25 published novels, 11 are on medical themes. Liston lives in Santa Barbara with his wife Jean.

Index

A

ADH 46
Aeschylus 48
Alcoholics Anonymous (AA) 18, 32, 120–128, 140
Alcohol (Ethanol) 41–47
  as anaesthetic 42
  breath and 45
  consciousness and 85–91
  as depressant 42
  effects of 41–47
  high 42
  history of 41
  Japanese and 47
  metabolization 46
  nature of 41
  reasons for drinking 43
  sleep and 9
  thirst and 67
  women and 64
ALDH 46
Amygdala 85
Anecdotes
  bridge 78
  doctor and phone call 15
  drunk in hotel 43
  drunk in theater 32
  drunk on train 61
  groceries stolen 61
  housewife's dinner 30
  John and Marsha 71
  Korean War veteran 99
  neighbors Ed and Bill 83
  superbowl game 34
  woman goes bowling 34
  writer at party 67
Anesthesia 153
Antabuse 46
Axons 51

B

Baars, Dr. Bernard J. 89
Baddeley, Alan D. 84
Bailey, Sonya and Christopher 93
BAL 67
Basetti, Narayan 113
Benzodiazepines 167
Binge drinking 60, 153
Blackouts
  abruptness of 57
  aloneness and 61
  areas for further studies 161
  bartenders and 76
  characteristics of 36, 54
  college students and 34, 60
  consciousness and 78–180
  curtailed consumption 66
  dealing with 74
  defined 54
  detection difficulties 58, 67
  drunkenness and 58
  ethical problems in testing 152
  fatigue, role of 9, 60
  food, importance of 44
  frequency of 33
  guilt and 14
  ignorance of 2, 35, 40, 67, 139,

154
murder and 96, 97
nature of 6, 96
need to recognize 67
as new disease 39
student's question 1
testing for 72
travel and 142
Bolen, George L. 106–130
Brain
alcohol and 45
researchers defined 155
Breathalyzer Test 74, 149
Brooks, Foster 139

C

Caron, Leslie 98
Chervu, Drs. Rao and Shanta. *See* **Cox, Paul**
Coats, Mildred 164
Colucci, Rita 63–93
Consciousness 78–91
alcohol and 81
defined 79
role of memory 80
stream of 80
Cowlin, Judge Henry L. 132
Cox, Frank and Mary. *See* **Cox, Paul**
Cox, Paul 16–19, 28, 57, 59, 62, 81, 82, 95, 105–128, 134–137
Crosby, Gary 32
Curl, Shaun 95

D

Date rape drugs 56, 159, 167–169
Deeble, Marjorie E. 94
Dendrites 51
Dissociative amnesia 139
Drinking problem 31
Drug Enforcement Administration 95
DSM-IV TR 139, 159
Dudley, Joyce 135

E

Edwards, Robert Mark 94, 103, 137
EEG 91, 161
Eichenbaum, Howard and Cohen, Neal J. 20–29, 50
Emotional memory 102
En bloc blackout 141
Ether 41, 55, 154
Euripides 12

F

Fadeout 15, 56, 144
False memories and confessions 126
***Father Goose* 98**
Faulkner, William 80
Fekete, Dick 95, 103
Ford, Charles Watson 134
Fragmentary memory 15, 145
Freberg, Stan 71
Freudian theory 76, 124, 159

G

GABA 55, 154, 169

Gauger, Gary 95, 131–137
Glutamate 52, 54
Goodwin, Dr. Donald 33, 141–151
critique of 145–146, 154, 157
Grant, Cary 98
Greene, Shecky 32
Grossman, Lt. Col. Dave 100
Grundberg, Ilo 164

H

Halcion 56, 164
Henry M. 20–29, 35, 54, 61, 66, 76, 78, 81
current events and 25
description of 20, 22
history of 20–23
importance of 20
length of memory 23
linked to blackouts 28
memory formulation 21
time, concept of 23
***High Society* 167**
Hilts, Philip J. 23
Hippocampus 21, 27, 52, 85, 151, 156, 169
Huff, Harold 63

J

James, William 49
Dr. Jekyll and Mr. Hyde 92
Jellinek, E. M. 140
Johnston, Arati Chervu 113
Joyce, James 80

K

Kahn, Kenneth 113
Kelly, Gene 16, 109
Kelly, Grace 168
Korean War 99

L

Lashley, K. S. 49
Law
blackouts and 130
detecting false claims of 136
identifying blackouts 137
need for standards 138
punishment and the 131, 138
special status and 6
unanswered questions 133
LeDoux, Joseph 82
Lopez, Jesus Belen 134
Loy, Myrna 64

M

Malingering 7, 36, 71, 91, 135, 148, 152, 159
Marshall, S.L.A. 100
Memento *27*
Memory
described 49, 51
emotional 102
fatigue and 8
formation of 51
history of studies 49
loss of 11–13
role in consciousness 81
role of 48
state-dependent 153
types of 6, 51
Miller, Randall E. 133

Morning after 67, 122, 165
MRIs 35, 49, 91
Murphy, Audie 100

N

Neimond, Bryce 87
Neuron 52
Neuroreceptor 52
Neurotransmitter 52, 85, 169
Newbury, Michael. *See* **Colucci, Rita**
***New York Times* 6, 118**
NMDA 52, 85, 154, 161, 169
working memory and 85
Nolan, Christopher 27

O

O'Brien, Devon 93
Operant conditioning 103
Outlaws gang 133

P

Pack, Gary W. 133
Pass out 8, 11, 30, 36, 45, 66, 76, 143
PET scans 35, 49, 91
Powell, William 64
Price, Kevin 5–13, 19, 37, 57, 59–77, 66, 102, 130–138, 146–172
at party 5
background 6
blacking out 5
head-on collision 5, 11, 74
life today 13
Psychology
critique of 156–164
defined 155

R

Reid, James Edward 94, 103, 137
REM sleep 60
Rohypnol 56, 159, 167–171
Rubin, Andrew 106–127
Rules for blacking out 45, 59–65

S

Schneider, James 133
Schoff, Jr., Steven 93, 103, 137
Scoville, Dr. William 21
Simpson, O. J. 113
Sinatra, Frank 167
Stevenson, Robert Lewis 92
Substance intoxication 139
Sweeney, M.D., Donal
career path of 2
relationship to Paul Cox 105
Sweeney, Ph.D., Daniel S. 68
Symptom Validity Test (SVT) 136

T

***The Thin Man* 64**
Triazolam 166

U

Ungar, Morton and Doris 164
Ungerleider, Dr. Leslie 85
The Upjohn Company (Pharmacia) 164

V

Vietnam War 100
Violence
against women 62–65, 104
in War 99

W

Weapons
firing in war 99
Weber, Dr. David 108
White, Aaron M. 34
Wholey, Dennis 31
Woodward, Ph.D., John H. 46
Working memory 11, 54, 68, 82–97, 130, 157
described 82–91

Y

Yahoo.com 35